Make some noise!
Jason Van Orden

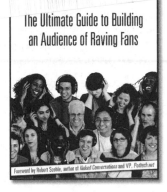

The Ultimate Guide to Building
an Audience of Raving Fans

Foreword by Robert Scoble, author of *Naked Conversations* and VP, Podtech.net

by Jason Van Orden

Published by:
Larstan Publishing Inc.
10604 Outpost Dr., N. Potomac, MD 20878
240-396-0007 ext. 901
www.larstan.com

PRINTED IN THE UNITED STATES OF AMERICA

10 9 8 7 6 5 4 3 2 1

Design by Mike Gibson for the Love Has No Logic Design Group
(http://www.lovehasnologic.com)
ISBN, Print Edition 978-0-9776895-5-2
Library of Congress Control Number: 2006924720
First Edition

"Getting your podcast noticed is becoming more difficult as more become available, Jason does an excellent job of showing podcasters specific and low- or no-cost ways of ensuring your podcast gets the audience it deserves quickly! This book goes much deeper than the typical 'get your podcast listed in all the directories' and guides readers through the less known, yet important steps to grow your audience."

Tim Bourquin, Founder, Portable Media and Podcast Expo / www.podcastexpo.com

"What would you pay to have a top expert in Podcast Marketing walk you (or your staff) through every single step of the Podcast Marketing process? Thousands? Would it be worth it? Yes! Do you need to? No! Hand them a copy of this book and expect results, because they will happen. Jason has held nothing back and I honestly can't believe he is selling this treasure—at any price."

Paul Colligan / www.theBusinessPodcastingBible.com

"A must-read for anyone serious about promoting his/her podcast."

Scott Fletcher, Podcheck Review / www.podcheck.com

"Jason's book has vital information every podcaster should know about getting their name out and gathering listeners to their show!"

Brian Ibbott, Coverville / www.coverville.com

"This is the most complete book on podcast marketing, or even basic e-marketing, I've ever read. It will be a great help to its readers—a must read."

-Gary Leland, Founder, Podcast Pickle: The First Podcast & Vidcast Community / www.podcastpickle.com

"People say any job is easy if you have the right tool. To this I add, 'But you have to know how to use the tool.' Jason's book shows you where the tool shed is, which tools are the best, and how to use each one."

Dave Jackson / www.schoolofpodcasting.com

"Promoting Your Podcast is *the* source for all the knowledge you need to get more subscribers for your podcast. From common-sense tips to often-overlooked promotional avenues, save yourself hours of scouring the 'net and buy this book! I wish it had been around when I was just starting out."

Joseph Nilo, Mac Pro Podcast / www.macpropodcast.com

"Jason's easy-to-follow tutorials on all things podcasting were my first stop when starting my own podcast. Following Jason's lead helped me to avoid many of the pitfalls that plague most novice podcasters… This book should be in the library of anyone who takes podcasting seriously."

Fred Johnson, Author, Global Mobile: Connecting without walls, wires, or borders / www.globalmobileonline.com

"Jason reveals the secrets of driving loads of listeners to your podcast, show after show."
                                                                    KFC, Podchick / www.podchick.com

"Jason is one talented individual. I've been involved in video and audio production for 30 years, and yet I'm learning valuable lessons from Jason... If you want to learn not only how to record quality podcasts but also become successful in creating an audience, Jason is the guy to learn from."
                            Art Juchno, Senior Media Specialist / University of Wisconsin-Stout

"Your information and knowledge help me quickly build my listeners and syndicate my podcast worldwide. Thank you, Jason. We couldn't have done this without you."
                            David Martin, Founder & CEO, PlanIt Podcast and Get It Planet

"If only spiritual enlightenment got people to listen to podcasts! The next best thing is Jason Van Orden. Follow his guidelines and you'll be on the path to podcasting prominence."
                    Avery Kanfer, Host, The Dalai Lama from Brooklyn Show / www.brooklynguru.com

"Jason's straight talking, easy to understand advice has helped me promote my podcast to more people than I thought possible. Thanks Jason!"
                                            Michael Boll, Host / www.autismpodcast.org

"Whether it is creating a podcast from scratch or discovering new ways to attract listeners, Jason has 'been there, done that'... it is nice to be able to get the information I need from one source without having to constantly consult the geek speak and acronym dictionaries."
                        Ken Wells, Producer, It's All About Marta (and me) / www.iaamam.com

"Your information is easy to chew, and invites serious fun without all the technical headaches for beginners."
                            Gary Goin, Minister of Music, Lighthouse Assembly of God

"After listening to Jason's podcast, I began using the principles he outlined. The number of listeners to our podcast went through the roof! I started podcasting as a hobby, but now I'm making money with it, too. Thanks, Jason!"
                                            Kevin Harter, Tasty Pods / www.tastypods.com

"I have several new industry contacts and have also increased my listenership to the thousands. Thank you Jason! All your hard work has made my job easy."
                                                            Cat Dumas, Creepycast

TABLE OF CONTENTS

THE TEAM

Editorial Directors John Persinos and Anne Saita
Contributing Editor Johnathan W. Holasek
Creative Director Michael Gibson
Production Manager Rob Hudgins

Group Publisher, Book Division Eric S. Green
COO Stan Genkin
CEO Larry Genkin

LARSTAN
PUBLISHING

FOREWORD

Robert Scoble, author of *Naked Conversations* and VP, Podtech.net

People who are into producing podcasts ask me all the time, "How do I get more traffic?" The question may come from my success with Microsoft's video and audio podcasting site, `channel9.msdn.com`, which has more than a million unique visitors. Or it may come from my new company, Podtech.net. Yet, I didn't really have a good answer until I read this book.

That's when it dawned on me that there's no one thing that'll guarantee you more traffic. It's doing dozens of seemingly little things that gets you noticed. In turn, you'll move up in search engine rankings and be more easily found on iTunes and other popular podcast directories. And, ultimately, you'll connect with an ever-broadening audience of avid listeners, which is what this great medium is all about, right?

This book provides the tactics to do just that, while also maybe settling the fundamental question that isn't quite as easy to address: Why are you doing a podcast in the first place?

That's why I hate it when people just ask me for traffic tips. I don't look at blogging or podcasting as an algorithm to create or crack or something mechanical. It's a human endeavor where you're trying to communicate something to other people. The tactics just let you communicate with more of those people. So the question I like to ask in response is this: "What makes you different?"

After all, you'll be competing with hundreds, possibly even thousands, of other people who have the same microphones, same computers, and the same book in their hands as you do. So, why should I pay attention to you? What are you doing that's exclusive? Different? Funnier? Sexier? Sillier? More serious? Higher quality?

Here are some steps I go through to make sure I'm able to answer those questions:

1. **Ask yourself, 'Who are you?'** I will reflect on some basic, but overlooked aspects of this business: What drives me? What am I passionate about? What will keep me doing a podcast a year from now when the thrill has worn off? What resources do I have access to that other people don't? (For instance, at Microsoft I had access to people who built the products that hundreds of millions of people use.) You might have access to an interesting community of doctors, or you might be a plumber who rebuilds bathrooms for the rich and famous. I write these down. Even someone with a seemingly boring job can come up with a great podcast. There's a trucker who does a podcast as he drives across country in his 18-wheel truck.

2. **Brainstorm search-engine keywords.** Say you're a plumber who works in Seattle, Washington. How will people find you on Google or Technorati? I doubt it'll be by searching for "cool joe smith." No, it'll be looking for things like "Seattle plumber" or "toilet expert" or "shower replacement." There is no bad keyword; just write them all down. Then enter them into Google and see if you can find any others. By searching for "plumber" you might find something like "sewer repair." Write that down too. These are all useful.

3. **Take your list and prioritize.** Follow the directions in Chapter 4. Jason has done a great job explaining how to figure out the quality of your search terms. Be open to other terms you discover in this process, too.

4. **Come up with a great name for your podcast.** Make sure you read Chapter 1 that shows how to use the keywords you discovered—that'll be important. For instance, naming something "Joe Smith's Wonderful Podcast" won't get you found on search engines nearly as well as "The Seattle Plumbing Show." Why is that? Well, even if you are lucky and get good rankings, people may assume that Joe Smith isn't a plumber and will just skip his entry. The Seattle Plumbing Show, however, explains exactly what it's about (and is far, far more likely to get listed under "Plumbing" or "Seattle").

5. **Become an authority on your topic.** This is hardest to do because demonstrating authority is subjective, not objective. But there are some simple things to do. For instance, are you linking to lots of other cool sites and podcasts that are like your own? If you're a plumber, for instance, and you find another cool plumbing site, I'd link to it and offer it as yet another great resource for plumbers. You've demonstrated you know where to find great sites while displaying a passion for your topic (and, by using one of your keywords, you've helped your podcast get found on search engines).

6. **Take it a step further.** I tell other bloggers that the best thing they can do is make a podcast or a videoblog. Why? Because what you want is to communicate to your audience what you're passionate about, right? If you care about politics, don't you want lots of other people who care about politics to listen to your podcast? Now, who's going to be most likely to be seen as an authority -- someone who has audio interviews with candidates, debates with friends and photos from campaign speeches, or someone who just has a text blog? Even if it is well written, the blog with audio, video, photos and an enticing name will see faster traffic growth than one that just is text. You can take that to the bank!

7. **Find invisible networks and join in.** Here's what I mean: I belong to a video blogger's mailing list over on Yahoo groups. If you read our mailing list it might seem to be only a small list of a

few dozen people. But, that list keeps getting quoted in press from Business Week to Wired magazines. Why is that? Well, journalists and other big-name bloggers, podcasters and video bloggers lurk there. All you have to do is ask or help answer a question and mention your video blog and you might find you're getting linked all over the place. Unless you read a book like this one, or come to a conference where you find one of the participants on the list, you might never have known that such a mailing list existed—or that a it could also be a boon to your podcast.

8. **Make cool-looking business cards and visit conferences your favorite podcasters attend.** We've been to Podcast Hotel, Gnomedex, DEMO, LIFT, PopTech, Consumer Electronics Show and many, many other conferences. At each one we've found at least a few famous podcasters. Taking them out to dinner after the show both lets you pick their brains and get your face in front of them. Take advantage of such networking opportunities and always carry your business cards bearing your podcast name, URL and subtitle.

9. **Take time to occasionally rethink everything you're doing.** The most popular search terms in your category might change over time. iTunes might be featuring other podcasts more than yours. Look at how your competition gets noticed. And keep coming up with fresh and exciting content.

If you're reading these words you're already excited about the industry's prospects. I am, too. I quit my job at Microsoft to join a small Silicon Valley startup, PodTech.net, specializing in audio and video blogging. You'll find me following every single one of the tips discussed in detail in *Promoting Your Podcast.* (And, if you discover other ways to get noticed, I'd love to trade tips with you and Jason—the journey you're on is a process of small steps, and it'll be rare that you find one big thing that'll get you noticed). Email me at robertscoble@hotmail.com.

Good luck, and I'll be looking for your podcast to rise up in the rankings on iTunes and Technorati!

AN AUDIENCE OF OCEANIC PROPORTIONS

"How do I attract more listeners or viewers to my podcast?" Of all the questions I hear from podcasters, this is the one that is asked more than any other. Whether beginner or pro, independent or corporate, we all share the same desire—to expand our audience. It doesn't matter if your goal is purely profit or some good old-fashioned ego gratification, you want a bigger audience. OK—maybe it's just me that wants ego gratification. I'm big (headed) enough to admit it. In any case, who doesn't want more listeners?

YOUR OWN PODCASTING SENSEI

What?! You don't have a podcast yet? Then you need to read my book, *Podcasting 101*. Podcasting is a lot of fun. Anyone can start their own talk show and rant to the world without permission from a major network or the cost of transmitters and FCC fees (or fines for that matter). The hard costs of starting a podcast are very small.

There is, however, a bit of a learning curve. There are a lot of facets to creating a podcast and getting it online, such as formats, feeds, show notes, directories, microphones, web sites, bit rates, megabytes, bandwidth—the list goes on. Do you ever hit a point where you wish you had someone to show you how to do it once and then you could do it yourself? *Podcasting 101* will teach you all the necessary steps in everyday laymen's terms, without lapsing into any of that "geek-speak."

Or, if you want a hands-on multimedia podcasting tutorial that walks you through the process, step-by-step, and shows you how to create a podcast, check out my site www.PodcastingUniversity.org. You'll feel like you're looking over my shoulder as I create, publish and promote my podcasts.

You'll be happy to know that there are numerous no-cost strategies for marketing your podcast, especially if you know who your ideal audience members are, and create content that they want. Podcasting is a powerful way to attract and build a relationship with a targeted group of listeners who are highly passionate about your topic. Each of my own podcasts is based on this premise—*Podcasting Underground* for podcasters, *GothamCast* for New York City enthusiasts and *Internet Business Mastery* for Internet entrepreneurs.

This "niche" philosophy is your key to success as a podcaster, both in creating content and in marketing your show. Your job as a podcaster is to carve out your niche, make your voice heard and become an expert and celebrity to a mob of hungry fans. This principle has proven itself true to me time and time again, first playing in several bands as a would-be rock star, then as a web entrepreneur and now as a podcaster.

As a guitarist, I've played in several bands through the years. The most recent was an alternative rock band called Desmo, in which my wife was the singer. We played shows regularly and produced our own albums. We learned how to identify our ideal fans, where to target them and how to grab their attention to keep them coming back to the shows and buying our music.

In 2003, I left my full-time, steady and "responsible" job as a software engineer to pursue the life of an entrepreneur. I had to learn quickly how to use no-cost, grassroots, guerrilla techniques to market myself on- and offline. These no-cost strategies have helped me create successful web businesses, marketing information to highly targeted groups of people who are passionate about a given topic.

Now I'm a podcaster and podcasting consultant. I produce three shows of my own, each targeting a different niche. This book draws from my experience as an independent musician, an entrepreneur, an Internet marketer and a podcaster to show you how to build—and keep—an audience of loyal listeners, and even a few (hundred, or maybe even thousand!) raving fans. These same promotional strategies have led to months where my audience has literally doubled in size.

Too many podcasters get discouraged by the difficulty of landing a coveted "Top 50" spot on the front page of the iTunes podcast direc-tory. They are overwhelmed by the mainstream media podcasts that flood the scene. They get caught up in the popularity game of getting votes in the major podcast directories. Do not despair. There are myriad other ways to pinpoint your potential listeners and reel them in.

Sure, getting featured in one of the directories is a splendid thing and will bring in a nice spike of listeners. It's happened to me twice and I hope you have that experience as well. However, the way to continually build a consistent fan base is to create small streams of new listeners that add up to an audience of oceanic proportions. Your fans are out there waiting for you. I say "fans" because we'll discuss how to attract an audience of loyal listeners who eat up every show you create.

Now, get ready to make some noise!

WHAT ABOUT THE VIDEO MEISTERS?

Never fear. This book is written for promoting either audio or video podcasts. I will refer mostly to "listeners," but any of the strategies covered in these pages are just as applicable to video podcasts and attracting viewers.

DOTTING A FEW I'S AND CROSSING A COUPLE T'S

Before we dive into the marketing tips, I want to make some suggestions that will prove useful before you begin promoting your podcast. I want to be sure we get started on the right foot.

1. **Get Thee a Blog**

   Chances are you already publish your podcast to a blog and post show notes to it for each episode. If you don't, I suggest that you start using a blog now. I recommend Blogger (www.blogger.com) or Wordpress (www.wordpress.org). They're both free. The former is a service that hosts your blog for you. The latter is a program that you install on your own site. If you need hosting and a blog, then Libsyn (www.libsyn.com) is a great all-in-one solution.

   Not only does using a blog make publishing your podcast easier, it also comes with many promotional benefits. Using a blog plugs you into a social culture that is very conducive to creating buzz and promoting your site. Blogs are also much loved by search engines. Believe me: using a blog will make your podcasting and promotional duties much easier.

If you use Blogger, you'll need FeedBurner to make your feed podcast-ready (see #3 below). Blogger does not create a podcasting compatible feed by itself.

2. **Get a Running Start**

It's a good idea to get a few episodes under your belt before you start promoting. I say this for two reasons.

First, podcasting takes time. There are no easy shortcuts. Remember when, in grammar school, you wanted to learn to play an instrument? Your parents bought one and a few weeks later, you gave it up. The same syndrome applies to many podcasters. Make sure you aren't going to burn out before you really get going (this has been dubbed "podfading" by Scott Fletcher of Podcheck). Start promoting your podcast once you have some momentum to keep going. Besides, this book will get you so pumped to podcast that podfading won't even cross your mind. Plus, we all want to hear what you have to say.

Second, it can take a few episodes to hit your stride. You'll find your voice, tweak the content and improve the audio. You know what they say about first impressions. If you want to put your best foot forward, you might not want to tell the world about your podcast starting with episode numero uno.

I assume you'll have *at the very least* one episode posted before promoting your podcast. It sounds silly to say, but once there was a podcast that got voted to the No. 1 spot on Podcast Alley even though it had zero episodes! Go figure. Somebody had a lot of friends with optimistic hopes for their podcast. I guess they just knew it was going to be that good and voted for it preemptively.

3. **Burn Baby Burn**

I hesitate to get into this subject at such an early point because it gets a little heavy. So bear with me. Are you ready? Okay, take a deep breath. Here we go. Let's discuss… FeedBurner.

FeedBurner is a free service that supercharges your feed with features, such as subscription statistics and iTunes' podcast tags. If you're just getting started with your podcast, I highly recommend starting an account and "burning" your feed. It's easy to do and will prove helpful in tracking the results of your marketing efforts. Make your way to www.feedburner.com for instructions on how to get started.

If you already have an established podcast with a healthy-sized audience, and you are not already using FeedBurner, then starting now is a little tricky for one reason. After you burn your feed, FeedBurner gives you a new feed address.

This presents a problem if your original feed address already appears in the podcast directories and your subscribers' aggregators. Your original feed address will still work, but to take advantage of Feed-Burner's features, you want everyone to use the new feed address. It can cause discrepancies in your tracking and other complications if you have two feed addresses floating around cyberspace and being used by your subscribers.

I don't want to get too heavily into the details right now, but if you're in this position and still want to use FeedBurner, you have two choices.

A. Create a FeedBurner account and start using the feed address you're given. Switch it in the directories and start using it in your marketing instead of the original feed address. Tell your subscribers to switch to the new feed address and hope that they do. This won't be so daunting if your audience is still relatively small.

B. You can forward your original feed to FeedBurner. This is an advanced technique that requires getting your hands a bit dirty in technical stuff. In this case you would continue to use your original feed address, but your web site would forward any subscriptions to that feed to FeedBurner to measure your statistics. For more information, listen to episode #7 of *The Podcasting Underground* (www.podcastingunderground.com) and go to www.PodcastingUniversity.org/feedburner. You can also check with your web host about how to set up this forwarding (also called a redirect).

Alright! Enough already! Before I fry our brains (too late) with all this talk of burning feeds, let's get started promoting your podcast.

UPDATES. GET YOUR FRESH UPDATES.

Podcasting is evolving rapidly. It's only natural that some of the sites I refer to and points I mention in this book will change with time. However, I have exercised great foresight in preparing a web site where you can get updates to the information contained in this book. To get all the latest, check out www.PromotingYourPodcast.com.

AUTHOR'S ACKNOWLEDGEMENTS

SPECIAL THANKS GO TO...

...my wife and best friend, Melanie, for always encouraging me to pursue my passion,

...my mom who passed on to me a writing gene or two,

...my dad who passed on to me a teaching (and sarcastic humor) gene or two,

...Jenny McCharen who gave creative input and took fantastic photos for the cover,

...Mike Gibson for his creative direction and incredible design,

...Michael Carrino (www.dmcex.com), Sterling Farnsworth, Jeremy Frandsen, Doug Kersten and Mike Wiebner for their feedback on the content of this book,

...John Persinos and Anne Saita, my editors, who helped me sound more eloquent than I would have otherwise,

...Larry Genkin, Eric Green, Rob Hudgins and everyone else at Larstan who helped bring this book to fruition,

...and Tim & Emile Bourquin (www.podcastbrothers.com) for playing one of my comments on their podcast and indirectly connecting me with my publisher, who was listening that day (a true testament to how podcasting can connect people).

Secrets for Maximizing the Number of Listeners That Find You in the Podcast Directories

DON'T GET LOST IN THE NOISE

One of the most common ways for listeners to find podcasts is through podcast directories. Your podcast needs to appear in these directories. If you want to quickly jump-start your listener base with little effort, submitting to the top podcast directories is the way to do it.

You might be thinking, "Duh! I'm already doing that!" I'm not trying to insult your intelligence by pointing out the obvious. You may have already submitted your podcast to some directories.

But keep reading. I might point out some directories that you overlooked. Most importantly, I'm going to show you some very valuable tips that will increase the number of people who find your podcast in the directories and click through to your site to listen.

Even if you've already named your podcast, written a description for it and submitted it, you'll still discover some important tips to further boost the traffic you're getting.

If you've ever perused the directories (and when I say "directories," in this context I'm talking about those directories that focus on listing podcasts), you know that there are a grundle of podcasts out there. At last count there were at least 44,000. The ease of podcasting allows thousands of new would-be DJs to post their audio musings to the web every month. This has created a flood of audio data.

Fortunately, the number of podcasts listeners is growing even faster. These listeners will turn to established search engines and directories to help them find podcast content that interests them.

When the listeners come searching, you don't want to get lost in the noise. How will you stand out? How can you maximize the number of listeners who find and click through to your podcast? I'll show you.

WALK A DAY IN YOUR LISTENER'S SHOES

To get the most exposure, it's important to understand how your typical listener uses the directories to find your podcast. There are three ways that listeners find podcasts in the directories:

1. They browse by category.
2. They do a search for keywords related to topics that interest them.
3. They look at the lists of top-ranked or featured podcasts.

It's much easier to influence the results you get from #1 and #2, especially when you're just getting started. You'll get greater returns in the long run by concentrating on how your podcast appears in category browsing and directory searches.

Not that there's no benefit to #3, appearing in the top-ranked lists. I just don't recommend worrying about it early on. But for those of you who still yearn after this Holy Grail, let's take a brief look at what you have to do to get featured.

TONIGHT'S TOP TEN LIST

Most podcast directories have lists ranking the top 10, 50 or 100 podcasts or picks by the editorial staff. In addition to ranking charts, many directories have "editor's picks" and other similar ways of featuring podcasts on their front page. Landing one of these spots is very rewarding and attracts a lot of new listeners.

The top-ranked podcasts are usually based on votes, ratings, reviews or number of subscribers. If you build a loyal listener base and produce good content, you'll start to see people review and rank your podcast in the directories. Eventually, if enough listeners raise their hands on your behalf, your podcast could land in one of the featured lists.

When this happens, a beaming smile will hit your face and you'll have a desire to pat yourself on the back. It also makes for great bragging rights and a nice bullet point in your podcast's media kit or resume. I hope you have this experience at some point. But before you get all fired up and expect it to occur tomorrow, let's look at the realities of making this happen.

Considering there are tens of thousands of podcasts and limited space in these ranking charts and featured spots, your show has as much of a chance of getting ranked as a plow horse has of appearing in David Letterman's Top Ten (actually, that might be pretty funny, but you get my point).

The following points do not make up a fool-proof formula, but here are some things I've noticed about the podcasts that get featured:

- They are consistent in releasing quality content.
- They have a solid description and a good logo.
- They have earned a large audience over time with the right subject matter and wide appeal.
- They spend time regularly soliciting their audience to vote for, and rank, them in a specific directory.
- They have a large cult following (or their subject matter does) that was mostly gained before the podcast even started (e.g., *The Firefly Podcast, MuggleCast,* NPR podcasts, *This Week in Tech,* etc.).
- They're affiliated with someone who has a large list of customers or clients to market to outside of the podcast.

If you're not associated with a cult following, large media outlet or don't have a big list of customers, don't worry. It's still possible to get ranked or featured. Here are a few things you can do to increase your chances:

1. Be patient. Consistently create good content that you're passionate about. You'll probably need to have several episodes posted before you get featured. People will catch on and want to tell others.

2. Release new episodes regularly. Directories won't feature your podcast if it is stagnant.

3. Create an attractive logo for your podcast and include it in the podcast feed. Apple has created a special `itunes:image` tag to be included with your feed. I'll talk more about how to use iTunes' tags below. Here's what the image tag looks like inside of your podcast feed file.

   ```
   <itunes:image href="http://www.site.com/logo.jpg" />
   ```

   Many podcast directories other than iTunes look in your feed for a logo and use it. Having the right logo will make it more likely that directories will feature your podcast.

   Create a logo for your podcast feed that is:

   - In JPG format
   - 300 x 300 pixels in size
   - Professional and clean
   - Not an infringement of other's copyrights or trademarks

4. Ask your listeners to vote for, or rate you in, a specific directory. If you have done #1, then they'll be responsive. When your audience relates to you and is excited about your show, they will act.

   Pick one directory and focus on it. If you push getting ranked in one directory, it will have a more potent effect than if you try to get ranked in all of them, and then get results in none.

   It used to be most popular to get votes from your listeners at Podcast Alley. It was one of the earliest podcast directories and probably the first to implement a ranking system. However, I think its importance and traffic were diminished with the arrival of iTunes and Yahoo on the scene.

I prefer asking for reviews and subscriptions in iTunes. iTunes is the most popular and universal directory. The majority of my subscribers use iTunes. If I'm getting featured in a top-ranked list, it's a good place for it to happen. Next to that I would choose Yahoo.

5. If your podcast is affiliated with TV, radio, a popular web site or some other type of medium, use that to cross promote your podcast and ask your listeners to rate, or vote, for you.

6. If you have a list of customers that you can reach by snail or electronic mail, let them know about your podcast. Get them to subscribe and ask them to vote for, or rank, you.

7. "Host a television show for six years on an obscure cable channel, develop a huge cult following, then leave the cable channel and reunite a year later [on a podcast]."

This is a facetious quote from a speech by Leo Laporte, of *This Week in Tech,* at Podcast Expo 2005. Laporte was sharing his formula for creating a successful podcast. For most of us, this isn't practical. His show is consistently ranked in the top podcasts lists due to a large and faithful following from his cable television show.

You can see that getting featured isn't easy and will take consistent effort. There are plenty of other ways to consistently get listeners. It would be a mistake to put too much stock into getting featured.

What can you expect if you do get listed? It should get you a nice spike in listener traffic. It's hard to measure the results exactly since they can vary widely, but let's look at an example.

In November 2005, my podcast, *GothamCast,* was featured as "New and Noteworthy" on the front page of Yahoo's podcast directory. This case is unique since it's chosen by Yahoo's editorial team and not the listeners, but I think it has a similar traffic spike effect and will give you an idea of what could happen.

My show was displayed for one week on the front page. Over the week, I noticed that the average daily amount of audio being transferred from my site (based on bandwidth stats) increased by 4.5 times. Most of the bandwidth from my site is from the audio files being downloaded or streamed. This makes it a decent measurement of how many more people were listening to my shows.

Granted, I was using other means of promotion at the time as well, so not all of that growth can be credited to Yahoo. Before being featured, my weekly listener growth was steady, at a 10-20% increase. You can see that being featured resulted in a significant traffic boost.

However, I estimate that the percentage of people that converted into regular listeners was lower than I would get with other marketing methods. It's easy for someone to click the listen button in the featured listings, but it doesn't mean they're a targeted prospect that is likely to subscribe. Someone that finds and listens to your podcast after searching for keywords that interest them is much more likely to continue listening.

The New York Minute Show, another podcast from The Big Apple, was featured on the front page of the iTunes podcast directory. This resulted in enough new subscribers to land the show on the top 100 list for two weeks, peaking at #39. Rob, the podcast's creator, estimates this brought in as many as 3,000 new listeners.

As you can see, getting featured is a nice goal to achieve. If you produce quality content, it can happen. But in the meantime, let's talk about some more immediate and practical methods of promoting your podcast in the directories. The following tips will work regardless of how new or old your podcast is, or the size of your audience.

A STRATEGY FOR STANDING OUT IN THE PODCAST CROWD AS IF YOU WERE WEARING A POLKA DOT SHIRT WITH STRIPED PANTS

Now we'll take a look at how you can stand out in the crowd to get more exposure to listeners browsing categories and performing searches in the directories. Many podcasters don't give any thought to the tactics you're about to learn—and that's why they're missing out on streams of listeners.

These tips are based on my personal experience with search directories, as a web entrepreneur as well as a podcaster. Use these suggestions and more listeners will find your podcast. Can you feel your ego getting bigger already?

Here are the tools that you'll use to increase your podcast directory exposure:

1. A gripping podcast title
2. A keyword-rich description and subtitle
3. The keywords in your feed
4. Carefully chosen directory categories

HOW TO CHOOSE A NAME FOR YOUR PODCAST THAT WILL REEL IN LISTENERS LIKE HELPLESS LITTLE FISH

Have you spent some time browsing the podcast directories trying to look for new shows to listen to? I say "trying," because you've probably noticed how tough it can be to find something you like. Sure, they have categories, ratings and searches to help you, but sometimes you're just left staring at a list of names with no idea of what to listen to first.

This is where a good title can really help a podcast stand out. Consider that the name of your podcast may be the first and only exposure a potential listener has to your podcast.

SIDENOTE: If you have already chosen a name for your podcast, you can take advantage of useful tweaks—e.g., subtitles—to get more mileage out of your podcast's name. I'll elaborate on this later.

Your title only has a few seconds to accomplish two goals:

> 1. Give the listener an idea of what your show is about
> 2. Entice him to click and give it a try

This requires choosing a title that is meaningful, but still creative and alluring. The right mixture of these two elements will depend on your genre and audience.

Take a look at this list, from January 24, 2006, of business podcasts from Podcast Alley.

Current Section: Business

Podcast that cover business, finance, small business and other issues relating to the work world.

- 1. Manager Tools
- 2. Killer Innovations
- 3. Mad Money Machine
- 4. KarmaBanque Radio: The...
- 5. Media Artist Secrets -...
- 6. The SalesRoundup Podca...
- 7. The M Show
- 8. Across the Sound
- 9. The Indie Analyst Show
- 10. The Cranky Middle Mana...
- 11. the WORKING PODCAST
- 12. The Prosperity Show
- 13. Greater Good Radio
- 14. ideaPeddling
- 15. audio lightbulb
- 16. The Invisible Hand
- 17. Marketing For Mental H...
- 18. FourBitsWorth Podcast
- 19. Real Estate Insiders -...
- 20. Music Pro Show
- 21. The Marketer's Podcast
- 22. Diary of a Shameless S...
- 23. Venture Voice
- 24. BizSlap
- 25. BizzyCast: Smart ways ...

Glance down the list. Which podcasts catch your attention, based on the name? (Actually, maybe none of them do if you think business is boring, but stay with me here.)

Again, let's take a walk in your potential listener's shoes. People who are browsing this category will skim down the list and look for a name that jumps out and grabs their interest. By looking at the title, they want to know if the podcast is on the topic they're looking for. This is crucial if you're offering news, information or commentary on a niche subject.

The name *Manager Tools* tells you that if you're a manager or interested in management, this podcast is for you. You get an idea of what to expect from the title. Other titles that do this well include *The Sales Roundup Podcast, Real Estate Insiders, Music Pro Show* and *The Marketer's Podcast.* A meaningful title has a greater chance of getting clicked.

If the name also sounds interesting, it's even better. Take the title, *Media Artist Secrets*. I can tell this podcast is probably for anyone who works with creative media. In addition, the word "secrets" is exciting. *Diary of a Shameless Self-Promoter* is both an enticing and meaningful title. You can tell it's about promoting yourself. It's too bad the title gets cut off. Fortunately most directories list the entire title.

Now, consider titles like *The M Show, Across the Sound* or *The Invisible Hand*. These titles have no apparent meaning. They don't tell you anything about the podcast. It turns out that "the invisible hand" is a reference to Adam Smith's theory of economics—probably too obscure for most people. It sounds cool, but you can't expect someone to know what it means just by looking at it. Who knows? Some people might assume it's a reference not to Adam Smith's book *The Wealth of Nations*, but to Claude Rains' character in *The Invisible Man*. The podcast is not even about economics; it's about management.

If one of these shows belongs to you, I apologize for picking on you. But hey, you just got some free exposure in my book. All press is good press. Obviously, you're doing something right if you're in the featured lists to begin with. But take it from me: your show would get even more listeners with a better title.

Your title is most likely a listener's first exposure to your podcast. It needs to be both informative and gripping.

These podcasts could be well produced and informative. But if I'm not enticed to click through, I'll never know. Your title is most likely a listener's first exposure to your podcast. It needs to be both informative and gripping.

I know you prefer a creative or cute name for your podcast. However, if you want to entice as many new listeners as possible, choose a name that means something without requiring too much thought. If someone has to scratch their head and ponder what your name means, they won't click. They won't stop to figure out the clever little pun in your podcast's name that you thought was so darn cool. Remember: don't force 'em to think!

That said, there are times when an insider phrase works. For example, *For Immediate Release* is a common phrase used in press releases. Chances are that any public relations professional will recognize the phrase and realize the podcast is about public relations (and if they don't, they won't be working for me). This is universal enough to mean something to the target audience.

Let's take a look at a list of political podcasts from iTunes. In this case, a good title is even more important to stand out. You can see that this is just a long alphabetical list. You don't want to get lost in this noise.

Name	Artist	Genre
Politische Analyse von Heldenbahn	Unknown	Politics
Polling Station Podcast Premiere #1	Steve & Henry	Politics
Pop and Politics Radio	PopandPolitics.com	Politics
Porkchop's Political Oddcast.	Unknown	Politics
PounceOnline	Pounce Online Staff	Politics
Power Line	John Hinderaker, Sco...	Politics
ppm	greg patterson	Politics
Prime Minister's Questions	flipdown.com	Politics
PrimeTime Politics Podcasts	Unknown	Politics
Pro-Choice Radio [EXPLICIT]	Pro-Choice Radio	Politics
Progressive Patriots Fund Video P...	Russ Feingold, US Se...	Politics
Progressive Point of View	The Progressive mag...	Politics
ProjectVillage Fair Trade Podcast	Matthew Kleinrock	Politics
Property and Local Tax Division C...	Minnesota House of ...	Politics
PUB DEF VIDEO PODCAST	PUB DEF	Politics
Public Affairs Podcast	Jeff Berkowitz	Politics
Public Campaign Action Fund - Ads	Public Campaign Acti...	Politics
Public Citizen's Outrage of the Week	Unknown	Politics
Public Interest.co.uk	Unknown	Politics

Think of your title as a book title or headline. Publishers spend a lot of time formulating titles that sell. Magazine editors carefully choose headlines for the front cover. You must put the same thought into your podcast's title. It needs to jump out to get clicked.

When my co-host, Sterling, and I chose the title for our business podcast, *Internet Business Mastery*, we conducted research to find out that the phrase "Internet business" was one of the most commonly searched on our topic. Then we used it in the title. Make it easy for your potential listeners and let them know that you have what they're looking for.

Does your title mean something to your audience? Does it tell them what to expect if they listen? Will it stand out in a long list of podcasts and pull them in?

Here are seven specific tips for brainstorming a name for your podcast:

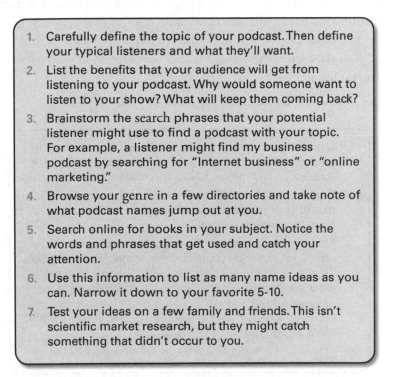

1. Carefully define the topic of your podcast. Then define your typical listeners and what they'll want.

2. List the benefits that your audience will get from listening to your podcast. Why would someone want to listen to your show? What will keep them coming back?

3. Brainstorm the search phrases that your potential listener might use to find a podcast with your topic. For example, a listener might find my business podcast by searching for "Internet business" or "online marketing."

4. Browse your genre in a few directories and take note of what podcast names jump out at you.

5. Search online for books in your subject. Notice the words and phrases that get used and catch your attention.

6. Use this information to list as many name ideas as you can. Narrow it down to your favorite 5-10.

7. Test your ideas on a few family and friends. This isn't scientific market research, but they might catch something that didn't occur to you.

I have a couple of comments concerning brand names. If your podcast is already associated with a recognized brand name, use it in your podcast's title (assuming you have the rights to do so). This will strengthen your brand and attract people to your podcast.

If you come up with a clever name and think that you'll "get the word out and make it a brand name," I hope you have a lot of time, manpower and money to put into it. Branding is a battle best left to large companies with lots of resources.

HOW TO GET RANKED AT THE TOP OF SEARCHES IN THE PODCAST DIRECTORIES

If you search the podcasts in iTunes for "Internet business," my podcast, *Internet Business Mastery*, shows up in the top results. A search in the Yahoo podcast directory (podcasts.yahoo.com) produces a similar outcome. For listeners to find your podcast, it needs to be in the top results when they search for words relating to your topic.

These search phrases are also called keywords or key phrases. These are the words that potential listeners will search for to find a podcast like yours in the directories. If your podcast is about pro baseball, then you want it to show up at the top of searches for phrases like "pro baseball" or "major league."

Three steps can help make this happen:

1. Use the one or two most important words/phrases in your podcast title, if you can. I'll show you a little trick for squeezing them in, using a subtitle format.

2. Use the key phrases in your podcast description. This is part of your feed and something that some directories have you enter when you submit.

3. Forgive me if I get a bit technical here. You should also use the keywords in your feed in the <itunes:keywords> tag. This is a part of your podcast feed that tells iTunes what your keywords are. Some other directories also use this. I'll talk about this some more later in the section called iTunes' Podcast Feed Tags. You can find more information on this here:

    ```
    http://phobos.apple.com/static/iTunesRSS.html
    ```

This is an example of what it looks like in your feed file:

```
<itunes:keywords>
internet,business,online,marketing,entrepreneur,ebay,tips
</itunes:keywords>
```

Let's talk about some tools that can help you choose your keywords.

THE SECRET TO FINDING GOOD KEYWORD PHRASES

As a web entrepreneur, I've built many sites. I've also worked to get those sites ranked at the top of the search engines. To do this, I conduct extensive research to find the most popular keywords that people search for and then use those phrases on my web pages. You want to use a similar strategy to get your podcast ranked in the podcast directories.

Here are a few tools that I use to brainstorm lists of keywords and determine which are searched for the most:

- https://adwords.google.com/select/KeywordToolExternal
- http://inventory.overture.com/d/searchinventory/suggestion/
- http://www.nichebot.com

The last one is my favorite. It gives you a statistic called "count" that tells you the relative popularity of a key phrase. The higher the count, the more it gets searched for in search engines.

Enter a phrase that describes your topic and these tools will return suggestions of similar phrases for which people search.

KEYWORD/PHRASE	COUNT	PAGES	COMPETITION	RATIO
baseball (click for related lateral results)	6,474,815	454,000,000	392,000,000	60.54
baseball betting (click for related lateral results)	1,864,526	8,820,000	1,060,000	0.57
major league baseball (click for related lateral results)	500,990	59,100,000	37,800,000	75.45
baseball bats (click for related lateral results)	469,953	17,300,000	2,540,000	5.40

For example, take a look at the results for the word "baseball" from Nichebot.

This will help you brainstorm good keyword phrases. I also suggest reading through the listings for other podcasts similar to yours, to get ideas for your description and keywords.

I have one more tidbit of keyword wisdom. It's easier to be ranked for two- or three-word phrases than for a single-word phrase. It will be harder to compete for the word "baseball" than for the phrase "pro baseball." Keep this in mind when choosing your phrases.

If you take a little time to come up with good key phrases, you'll show up higher in searches and attract more listeners.

THE SECRET WEAPON: YOUR SUBTITLE

I'm going to pick on myself now. I've mentioned one of my podcasts called *GothamCast*. The podcast is about New York City. Gotham is a nickname for New York City, where I live.

After the podcast was underway, I discovered this really wasn't the best name. Even though it had flare, the meaning was not clear. Not everyone knows that Gotham is New York City. When I say my podcast's name, some people think of Batman. Others think it has to do with gothic culture. Never assume too much knowledge on the part of your audience.

I admit, I came up with the name in a hurry while sitting in a restaurant on the Upper East Side and writing on a napkin. I was probably thinking more about my brunch than the title. I need to follow my own advice more often.

I was sort of stuck with my name, since I already owned the web address GothamCast.com. I really didn't want to go through a complete name and web site change. But then I thought of a solution. Now it's going to be your secret weapon—a subtitle.

I wanted to find a way to use the phrase "new york city" in my title. This was my main key phrase. I figured that the directories would rank me higher if the phrase was in the title. So I changed the name to *GothamCast: A New York City Experience.*

I did the same thing with my business podcast. I changed the title to *Internet Business Mastery: The Art of Online Marketing and Entrepreneurship.* This allowed me to insert additional keywords into my title, such as "online marketing" and "entrepreneurship." Now we rank well for those phrases, too.

I changed the title in the <title> element of the <channel> tag in the podcast feed. If you use a blog service or software such as Wordpress, Blogger or Libsyn, then changing the title in your blog settings will change your feed.

For Wordpress, click the *Options* tab in your admin panel and change the *weblog title* field.

For Blogger, log in to your account then select the blog you want to change. Click the *settings* tab. Change the *title* field.

For Libsyn, log in to your account then click on the *settings* tab. Change your title in the *blog page/podcast title* field.

This is what it will look like in the feed:

```
<channel><title>
Internet Business Mastery: The Art of Online Marketing and
Entrepreneurship
</title>
```

Notice I don't use the <itunes:subtitle> tag for this. This is usually used for a description of your podcast.

After making these changes, the title will eventually show up in the podcast directories, once they check the feed again. Now let's take the keyword thing one step further.

HOW TO WRITE A POWERFUL AND ENTICING DESCRIPTION FOR YOUR PODCAST

Ask yourself these questions: "Why would someone want to listen to my podcast? When there are so many podcasts to choose from and only 24 hours in a day, why would someone want to give up some listening time to hear my podcast?"

Your description needs to answer these questions. Tell your potential listeners why they want to listen to your podcast. What will they get from listening? What can they expect? Will they be entertained? Will they be informed?

Here are additional suggestions to consider when writing your description:

- Quote a raving fan about why they love your show.
- Use your keywords in the description.
- Include statistics as to how many other people listen.
- Include your web address. Some directories don't make it obvious how to get to your web site. If you put it in the description, it will be obvious.
- Tease the listener's curiosity.
- Pay attention to your first sentence. This needs to clinch the reader. Also, some directories may show only this sentence as a summary in some of their listings.

Here is the description for *GothamCast: A New York City Experience.*

n. *GothamCast:* 1. Your guide to Gotham, aka New York City 2. A vicarious slice of The Big Apple 3. A virtual venue for indie music from the NYC area. 4. An audio blog chronicling the discovery of Manhattan and its environs by a transplant from the west

I'm trying to be a little creative and original by putting it in the format of a dictionary entry. Notice how it gives you an idea of what to expect.

It's a vicarious NYC experience, a guide to the city including indie music from the area. I also point out my point of view as a relative newcomer to the city. This tidbit sets me apart and gives me a unique angle.

Also, notice that the description uses the keywords "new york city," "nyc," "the big apple," "gotham" and "manhattan." This will increase my chances even more of being ranked highly for my keywords.

EPISODE TITLES ARE HEADLINES, TOO

You can use these same tips to write the title of each episode. If a potential listener clicks through to your podcast in a directory, they will see a list of your most recent episodes. Think of each episode's title as a headline, as well.

Grab the person's interest. Make them want to take the next step to listen or subscribe. You need to keep them moving forward until they become a loyal audience member.

If you're using a blog to publish your podcast, the episode title is the same as the title for the blog entry for that episode. This is what directories will list.

Using the right keywords is important here as well. Some directories include individual episodes in search results. You will also read later about how the right title for each blog post will lead to higher rankings in search engines, such as Google.

The directories also may list all or some of the show notes as an episode description. This is pulled from the blog post. The first couple sentences are equally important in grabbing a listener's interest.

SUBMITTING TO MULTIPLE CATEGORIES

When you submit your podcast to a directory, you'll probably be asked to assign it to a category. Keep in mind, you may be able to submit to more than one category. Don't shortchange yourself here. iTunes lets you submit up to four additional categories besides your main one.

Use your imagination. What other categories would your podcast fit under? The more places your podcast appears, the more likely you are to be found.

For example, I submitted *Internet Business Mastery* to the business, marketing and education categories.

Brainstorm a little and be creative, but don't trick people. Don't post in a category that doesn't apply. People resent the "bait and switch."

IMPORTANT WARNING CONCERNING LONG FILE NAMES

Avoid long filenames when you create your MP3 or other audio file. A filename that includes podcast name, episode number and date is adequate. For a while I experimented with using a few description keywords about the episode when I named a file. This made for a very long filename. I figured if Windows can handle it, why not?

Well, I then discovered that the player in the Yahoo Podcast Directory wouldn't play those files. That was a problem, considering they'd just put my podcast, GothamCast, on the front page as New and Noteable and traffic was coming in. I had to hurry and release a new episode with a shorter filename so that when someone hit the listen button, it would work. I don't know why this was a problem, but the moral of the story is it is safest to keep your filenames from being too long.

GETTING THE MOST BANG FOR YOUR BUCK WHEN SUBMITTING TO PODCAST DIRECTORIES

Eventually, you should list your podcast in as many directories as possible. To get you started, I've listed below the most popular directories. If you submit to these, you'll get the majority of the benefits from directories. After you submit to the most popular directories, you could set a goal to submit to a certain number of other directories each week or month.

> In fact, submitting your podcast to iTunes, with the right title and keywords, is the single most important thing you can do to start getting listeners today.

Here are my top suggestions for podcast directories to submit to, ranked by importance:

A. **iTunes**

If you only list your podcast in one directory, this must be it. In fact, submitting your podcast to iTunes, with the right title and keywords, is the single most important thing you can do to start getting listeners today. Apple has, by far, the most MP3 players on the market, and it also has the largest directory of podcasts available online. Apple seems to own the podcast market on and offline. It's the 800-pound gorilla.

Most podcasters I talk to agree that iTunes brings more subscribers to their podcast feed than any other podcast directory. I don't see any sign of this slowing down. All three of my podcasts gained listeners fast from iTunes, as soon as I submitted to the directory. Today, at least 70% of my subscribers are using iTunes to subscribe.

To submit your podcast to iTunes, you must have it installed. You'll need to be signed up for, and logged into, a free iTunes account. Open iTunes and go to the Music Store. Click on the podcasts link and then submit a podcast.

It can take a little while to show up in this directory. You may need to wait up to a week or two. If you still aren't showing up, make sure that you are using a valid feed and then contact iTunes podcast support.

iTunes' Podcast Feed Tags

I have to slip into geeky feed talk again for a moment.

You should be aware that iTunes has some special tags for you to use in your podcast feed. A tag is just a piece of information that describes your podcast to iTunes (e.g., the iTunes category, whether it contains explicit content, identity of the author, etc.).

These tags tell iTunes how to list your podcast in its directory. For more information from Apple on the iTunes tags, go here:

```
http://phobos.apple.com/static/iTunesRSS.html
```

If you have no idea what I'm talking about or are not sure how to change your feed, then the easiest way to include iTunes tags is to use the free FeedBurner service (www.FeedBurner.com). They take care of it for you with their SmartCast feature.

Here is how to use FeedBurner to add iTunes tags to your feed.

1. Go to www.FeedBurner.com and log in to your account (you'll need to register if you've not already done so).

2. Click on the name of the podcast that you want to add iTunes tags to

3. Click the *Optimize* tab.

4. Click the *SmartCast*™ button.

5. On this page you will see a variety of information that you can fill in for your podcast. This is the information that will be used to create the iTunes tags in your podcast feed. Make sure the checkbox marked *Include iTunes podcasting elements* is selected.

6. Choose the categories that apply to your podcast. Be sure to click *Use additional categories* to enter more than one category.

7. If you have a podcast logo image that you want to be displayed in iTunes and other directories, enter the web address to this image here. The image should be 300 x 300 pixels (JPEG format).

8. Enter your description and keywords using the tips I outlined before.

9. Enter the rest of the information. You can check Include "Media RSS" information and add podcast to Yahoo! Search. This is another place that FeedBurner will list your podcast.

10. If the SmartCast™ feature is not yet activated, press the activate button and then save your info.

B. Yahoo! Podcasts

If there is one company that can give iTunes a run for its money, it's Yahoo. Yahoo has shown a significant interest in, and long-term commitment, to podcasting.

Once you have submitted your podcast, you should go to your podcast listing and add tags to classify your show. This is another good place to use your key search phrases. It is one more way to increase the chances that you'll be displayed in searches for these phrases.

You'll need a Yahoo ID to submit your podcast feed. Submit to Yahoo here:

```
http://podcasts.yahoo.com/publish
```

C. Podcast Pickle (www.podcastpickle.com)

Podcast Pickle is not just a directory, but a community for podcasters. Its founder, P. Dilly, has become a minor celebrity in the podcasting world and works hard on his site. You also can create a profile page and participate in forums at the Podcast Pickle site.

You'll have to register (free) and log in to submit your podcast. Submit your podcast here:

```
http://www.podcastpickle.com/casts/add/index.php
```

D. Podcast Alley (www.podcastalley.com)

Podcast Alley is a pioneer among podcast directories. iTunes came along and, to a certain degree, overshadowed it. It's still a widely visited site, though. I get traffic from Podcast Alley on a regular basis.

The site is now owned by Adam Curry's Podshow. It will be interesting to see what happens with time. It's still a popular "hangout" and directory for "indie" podcasters.

Podcast Alley ranks podcasts based on monthly votes. It has become common for podcasters to ask listeners to vote for their show at Podcast Alley.

Not only do listeners vote at Podcast Alley, but they can also leave comments for the podcaster.

Submit to Podcast Alley here:

```
http://www.podcastalley.com/add_a_podcast.php
```

E. Podcast.net (www.podcast.net)

This is a directory that allows you to search by title and description, keywords, location, show host and episodes. There also are numerous categories and a list of the most recently added podcasts.

I see regular traffic to my site coming from this directory.

Submit your podcast here:

```
http://www.podcast.net/addpodcast
```

F. Podcast Bunker (www.podcastbunker.com)

According to their site, Podcast Bunker lists "only the best podcasts on the net." This is based on audio and content quality. Every listed podcast is hand-selected. It constantly checks its listings to make sure the links and feeds are current.

You'll be required to have a link back to Podcast Bunker to be listed. I would suggest having a link already up on your site when you submit your podcast. This will increase your chances of being selected. Podcast Bunker will not include podcasts that contain vulgar content. You should also have the iTunes tags in your feed.

In 2005, Podcast Bunker was featured in Time magazine's "50 Coolest Web Sites."

Submit your podcast here:

```
http://www.podcastbunker.com/Podcast/Podcast_Picks/
Podcast_ Submit_Form/
```

G. Transistr: formerly iPodderX (www.transistr.com)

Transistr is another popular podcatcher. The site and the software itself include a directory. It's a good idea to have your podcast included in this directory.

Submit your podcast here:

```
www.transistr.com
```

H. Odeo (www.odeo.com)

Odeo's focus has been unclear as time goes on. It originally seemed to have grand plans, but perhaps iTunes and Yahoo trumped it. In any case, it's still a nice directory with good features, and it's worth submitting to.

Again, you'll have to register and log in to add your podcast.

Submit your podcast here:

```
http://www.odeo.com/create/import-feed
```

I. Zencast (www.zencast.com)

This is a directory started by Creative, a company in second place to Apple in the MP3 player market.

Submit your podcast here:

```
http://www.zencast.com/contactus/submit.asp
```

J. Digital Podcast (www.digitalpodcast.com)

To submit your podcast, you'll need to register and log in to this site.

MORE DIRECTORIES TO SUBMIT TO

By submitting to the directories listed above, you'll have your bases well covered and get the majority of the benefit. But there are still a lot of other directories you can submit to.

More podcast directory listings mean more streams of traffic to your podcast, which add up to more listeners. It also means more links pointing back to your site, giving you better rankings in the search engines.

SUMMARY

Submitting your podcast to podcast directories is the quickest way to start building your audience. The iTunes Music Store and Yahoo Podcast Directory (podcasts.yahoo.com) get the most traffic and are the best place to start.

To maximize the number of listeners who find you, your podcast needs an enticing title that will reel people in. Your title is the first thing people see. It needs to make them want to hear more. Think of it as a headline for your podcast. If possible, you should include one or two keywords that potential listeners would search for to find a podcast like yours.

A description for your podcast is also listed in the directories. It should tell people why they want to listen to your show. The description needs to include search keywords as well. This will give your podcast more exposure when people search for those words in the podcast directories. If a keyword appears in your title and description, you are more likely to show up at the top of podcast directory search listings for that word.

Use the iTunes tags in your podcast feed. Many directories use this information when listing your show.

Multimedia Tutorials at PodcastingUniversity.org

For more help with the topics covered in this chapter, please visit: www.PodcastingUniversity.org/pyp/chapter1

You'll find multimedia tutorials on:

- Finding the best keywords for your title and description
- Using iTunes tags in your podcast feed
- Changing your podcast's title and description in the feed
- Submitting your podcast to iTunes and other popular directories

As well as further resources such as:

- A list of other podcast directories to submit to

...and more!

When is a Podcast a Blog? When it Gets You More Listeners.

DIRECTORIES, DIRECTORIES AND MORE DIRECTORIES

Blogs and podcasts share a lot in common. Chances are you're using a blog to publish your podcast to the Internet. In fact, your podcast is essentially just a blog with audio in the feed. So why should you limit yourself to submitting to podcast directories? You should take full advantage of the blog-like nature of your podcast. There are hundreds of great directories and publicity opportunities out there for blogs.

There are hundreds of great directories and publicity opportunities out there for blogs.

Even if being listed in a directory doesn't directly bring you new listeners, the more links you have pointing to your site, the higher you will be ranked in the search engines. Every directory you appear in creates another link back to your podcast.

Here are a few tips concerning blog directories:

- Use the same techniques you learned in the chapter on podcast directories when writing your description and keywords.
- Read the online submission forms carefully! Some directories ask you for your blog's web address and some ask you for the podcast feed address. Be sure to enter the right one.
- Wait until you have a few episodes released before submitting. Some of these directories review your site to be sure it provides regular content.

- A few directories can take some time before you are listed if their submissions are manually screened. It could even take a month, or more, for some. Be patient. Just get your info in now so you can start reaping the benefits sooner, rather than later.

- Some of these sites require you to place a link on your site back to them. I've indicated where this is the case in the list below. It's best to have the link up on your site before you submit.

To help you use your time wisely, I've listed some directory recommendations:

1. **BlogDigger**
   http://www.blogdigger.com/add.jsp

2. **Blogwise**
   http://www.blogwise.com/submit

   Submit your site web address, not your feed address. Submissions are manually screened.

3. **Blog Universe**
   http://www.bloguniverse.com/

   To submit to this directory, surf from the homepage to the category that is most relevant to your podcast, then click the *Add a Site* link. One obvious category to submit to is Podcast.

   All submissions are manually screened before being listed. The downside is that it takes time to get listed. The upside is that being listed is a more exclusive privilege. You have two choices, you can pay $1.99 to hurry things up (a small price to pay to get listed in under 72 hours), or you can just wait it out. If you're not paying, then you have to include a link to Blog Universe on your site.

4. **Blog Catalog**
   http://www.blogcatalog.com/blogs/submit_blog.html

5. **Blog Top Sites**
   http://www.blogtopsites.com/register.php

   Blog Top Sites has been getting a lot of traffic to its directory lately. This directory ranks blogs by the number of unique visitors they receive. The ranking is reset every week.

To be included in the directory's ranking, you have to insert a block of code in your site. This is how they measure your traffic. This also places a little graphic on your site that lists your current rank and links back to the directory.

I have to be honest. I haven't tried this one before. One problem I see is that podcast listeners don't visit sites nearly as often as blog readers do because the audio content comes to them. This means you won't get as much traffic as other sites, which will hurt your rank.

However, this might be worth trying if you also have written blog entries or other content that brings listeners to your site regularly. I've seen some podcasters using it.

6. **Bloggernity**
   http://www.bloggernity.com/cgi-bin/add.cgi

7. **Globe of Blogs**
   http://www.globeofblogs.com/register.php

8. **IceRocket**
   http://www.icerocket.com/c?p-addblog

9. **Blogarama**
   http://www.blogarama.com/index.php?show=add

   You'll need to register and log in to submit your podcast.

10. **Blog Explosion**
    http://www.blogexplosion.com

    To submit, you have to register and log in. Then click the *Add/Edit Podcasts* link. It takes 48-72 hours to get approved.

    This is a directory with a unique feature. You earn traffic credits by surfing other blogs. The more you surf, the more you get traffic. BlogExplosion also has a directory just for podcasts. There are numerous other features, as well as a community feel, to this directory.

This is just the beginning, but these are some of the most popular directories. There are dozens of others that you could submit to. If you really want some more quality time with the blog directories, try a search in Google for *blog directory* or *blog directories,* and that will turn up some more.

Maybe you're a perfectionist. Maybe you're a masochist. Maybe you just want more links back to your site. Even if no one ever looks at Bob's Directory of Blogs, it gives you a link. The search engines see those links to your site and rank it higher for relevant searches because it must mean your site is popular.

JUST WHEN YOU THOUGHT YOU'D SEEN THEM ALL—MORE MEDIA SEARCH ENGINES AND DIRECTORIES

The following directories index audio and video. They can also be sources of traffic and listeners. You should submit your podcast to each of them.

1. **Yahoo RSS Media Search**
   http://search.yahoo.com/mrss/submit?
   Yahoo has a search feature for audio (audio.search.yahoo.com) and another for video (video.search.yahoo.com). The link above allows you to submit your feed for inclusion in Yahoo's RSS media search engine. The search results appear to be largely based on blog post titles and show notes.

2. **Podscope**
   http://podscope.com/submiturl.php
   Podscope is a search engine for audio and video. Using speech recognition technology, they convert your audio into text and make it searchable. After submitting your podcast feed to Podscope, they will convert your audio to text and include it in their search engine. You can also insert a Podscope search box on your site.

3. **Podzinger**
   http://www.podzinger.com/register.jsp
   This is another search engine for audio and video. Similar to Podscope, Podzinger converts your audio to searchable text.

4. **Loomia**

   `http://www.loomia.com/addfeed`

   Loomia is an audio and video directory that helps listeners "find good stuff." Based on the content that users listen and subscribe to Loomia make recommendations that might interest them.

5. **SingingFish**

   `http://search.singingfish.com/sfw/submit.html`

   This is another audio and video search engine. They crawl web sites and index media files based on the content of the site.

6. **Blinkx**

   `http://ussubmit.blinkx.com/registration/`

   This is a video, TV and podcast search engine. To submit your content, go to the web address listed above. Click on *Begin*. Enter your information and then click *Next*. You'll be asked to upload media to their site. Instead, click on the link indicating that your files are already hosted on the Internet. Then click on the *I Have RSS* button. Enter your feed and then click on the audio or video button depending on what type of podcast you have.

YOU'RE BEING TRACKED, AND IT'S A GOOD THING

Do you like your podcasts fresh? Then take a look at `audio.weblogs.com`, which lists the most recent podcast episodes posted to the Internet. In addition to the podcast and blog directories that I've already mentioned, there are sites that track and list the latest entries in the blogosphere (that's a little Internet slang for you to drop at a party sometime) and the podosphere... er... the podcastosphere, or whatever they want to call it now.

Every time you release a new podcast episode, you can let the world know by informing... listing sites.

Directories list links to blogs, but these services track and list new entries in those blogs. Every time you release a new podcast episode, you can let the world know by informing these listing sites. Here are a few sites that track new entries to blogs and podcasts.

- www.weblogs.com
- www.technorati.com
- www.pubsub.com
- blo.gs
- www.blogrolling.com
- www.blogstreet.com

These sites are updated when they receive what's called a ping (that's some more Internet jargon for you, but don't use that at the same time as "blogosphere," or you might seem a little too geeky). When you post a new episode to your podcast, you send a ping to the tracking site to get your blog post listed.

Don't let the word ping scare you. This is techno-babble, but the idea here is rather simple. A ping is a way for two web sites to communicate across the Internet. That's all. Basically, your blog is telling the tracking service that there's new material on your site, so come and take a look.

There are two ways to ping the listing sites: you can use a pinging service or have your blog do it for you automatically. First, I'll show you the slow way. They say you should learn to do things the hard way first, right? Actually, this is good to know in case the automatic solution doesn't work on your blog platform, or you don't use a blog.

The following sites are helpful for sending pings to the most popular blog and podcast tracking services:

1. **Ping-O-Matic**
   http://pingomatic.com/

   When you go to the Ping-O-Matic site, you'll see a short web form and a list of directories to ping. First fill out the name of your blog/podcast (e.g., GothamCast). In the next, field type in your podcasts home page address (e.g., http://www.gothamcast.com). In the third field, type in the web address for your feed (e.g., http://www.gothamcast.com/feed/, http://feeds.com/podcastfeed/, http://feeds.feedburner.com/podcastfeed/, etc.).

   Make sure that all of the boxes are checked in the upper portion of the list, from *Services to Ping* down to *Specialized Services.* Then, under Specialized Services, check *Audio.Weblogs.* Click the *submit* button. You've just pinged the most popular listing sites. The next web page will show you the results from each site.

   You can save a lot of time in the future by bookmarking the link for the results page. It contains all the data needed to automatically submit the information you entered on the previous page. In the future, you will only need to click on the bookmark to send a ping for that podcast.

2. **AllPodcasts**
   http://www.allpodcasts.com/PingAll/Default.aspx

   This site pings a number of podcast directories and search engines, such as Odeo and Podscope. Simply enter your feed web address and click *Ping.* You will then see a list of the results, as well as, a *Bookmark This Ping* link. Click on the link and store a bookmark for the page it takes you to. This will save you some time in the future.

3. **Fresh Podasts**
   http://www.freshpodcasts.com/xmlrpc/client.php

   This is another site that lists the 100 most recent podcast updates. Go to the site and enter your podcast's name and feed address. Then click submit. If you look at their list of recent updates, you should see your podcast at the top.

Now you can let your pings fly through the blogosphere with the best of them. And don't forget to let your new Internet jargon fly with the geekiest of them.

HOW TO AUTOMATICALLY NOTIFY PODCAST & BLOG TRACKING SERVICES

Now that you've done it the hard way and have an appreciation for "what it was like when I was growing up," I'll show you the easy way. The good news is that most blogging platforms can automatically ping listing sites for you when you post a new episode. You don't have to visit any sites or submit any forms. It just happens behind the scenes without you lifting a finger.

Each blogging platform (e.g., Blogger, Wordpress, TypePad, etc.) handles pinging a little differently. Here's a list of addresses that you want your blog to ping each time you add a new podcast to your feed.

- rpc.pingomatic.com
- api.feedster.com/ping
- api.my.yahoo.com/rss/ping
- bulkfeeds.net/rpc
- ping.blo.gs
- ping.feedburner.com
- audiorpc.weblogs.com
- rpc.technorati.com/rpc/ping
- api.moreover.com/RPC2
- odeo.com/api/xmlrpc/1.0/ping
- services.podcasttags.com/ping/rpc.ashx

These are just some of the services to ping. You could easily find dozens more. This should get you the majority of the benefit, though. If you want to find more ping services, a Google search for *blog ping list* will prove fruitful. I have one word of caution. If you give your blog too many services to ping, it could really slow down the posting process.

Ping addresses are not like web addresses that you can visit in your browser. You enter them into you blog's ping configuration. I'll walk through how to set this up on the most popular blog platforms.

PINGING WITH WORDPRESS

1. Log in to your Wordpress admin panel.
2. Click on the *Options* tab.
3. Click on the *Writing* tab.
4. Scroll down to the *Update Services* heading. In this text box under this heading, enter the list of ping addresses from above.

Update Services

When you publish a new post, WordPress automatically notifies the follo
Services on the Codex. Separate multiple service URIs with line breaks.

```
rpc.pingomatic.com
api.feedster.com/ping
api.my.yahoo.com/rss/ping
bulkfeeds.net/rpc
```

PINGING WITH BLOGGER

Unfortunately, Blogger is not as flexible. You can only set it to ping weblogs.com. However, you can rest assured in your substandard pinging, knowing that a lot of tracking sites, directories and search engines watch weblogs.com for updates. To cover your bases better, you can ping by hand, as explained above. Here's how to set Blogger to ping *weblogs.com*:

1. Log in to Blogger.
2. Click on the name of the podcast you want to configure.
3. Click on the *Settings* tab.
4. Click on the *Publishing* link.
5. Next to *Notify Weblogs.com*, select *Yes*.

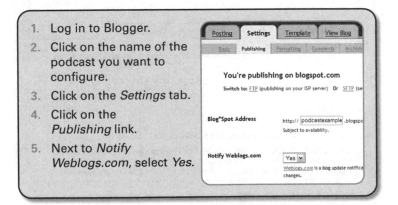

PINGING WITH TYPEPAD

As of the writing of this book, Typepad only allows pinging of blo.gs and weblogs.com. This will still offer some good publicity, but you might want to do the manual pinging described above as well. Here's how to configure pinging in Typepad:

1. Log in to your Typepad account.
2. Under *Your Weblogs,* click on the name of the podcast you want to configure.
3. Click the *Configure* tab.
4. Click the *Publicity & Feeds* link.
5. Under *Would you like to notify third-party services when you update your weblog,* click all the checkboxes and then *Save Changes.*

   There is one other option with Typepad. Go to the *Post* page and you will see a box below the *Post Body* textbox labeled *Send a TrackBack to these addresses.* Trackback is just another snooty tech word. You just need to know that the trackback box will work for sending pings from Typepad. When you save your post, a ping will be sent to the addresses you list in the box.

   Enter the ping addresses from my list above. You'll need to do this each time you save a new post. I suggest saving the ping in a text file. That way you can just copy it and paste it into Typepad.

| Weblogs |
| Manage | Post | Design | Configure |

Weblog Basics | Archiving | Categories | **Publicity & Feeds** | Preferences

Publicity and Feeds: Podcasting Underground

Publicity

Would you like your weblog to be public? ○ Yes ⦿ No

Public means that your weblog will appear on TypePad's Recently Updated list and directories, and anyone will be able to read your weblog. Marking your weblog as public is a great way to increase your site's traffic and gives more people the

PINGING WITH MOVABLE TYPE

1. Click on *Main Menu*, then choose the name of the podcast that you want to configure.
2. Click *Configuration*.
3. Click *Preferences*.
4. Click the link named *Publicity/Remote Interfaces/Trackback*.
5. Click each of the checkboxes in this section and enter the "ping addresses" listed above in the text box.

PINGING WITH LIBSYN

1. Log in to your Libsyn account.
2. Click the *Settings* tab.
3. Click the *Advanced* button.
4. Under the *Publishing* heading, check the box marked *ping when a podcast is added*.

This will ping audio.weblogs.com, odeo.com and podcasts.yahoo.com. You may also want to do some pinging by hand, to supplement.

SPECIALIZED BLOG DIRECTORIES

So far I've talked about blog directories in general. However, there may be blog directories dedicated just to your podcast's topic. For example, I found a directory that lists blogs about New York City. The directory is ranked high in Google when you search for "new york city blogs." I submitted GothamCast for listing, and now I regularly get traffic from that directory.

Do some exploring on the 'net and in the search engines to see if you can find any specialized blog directories for your topic. Then submit your podcast for listing. If you can't find one, you could always start one yourself. Who says you can't have a directory of blogs and podcasts about bottle cap collecting?

A LITTLE TRICK FOR BLOGGER USERS

This is a tip just for Blogger users that could get your podcast in front of more Blogger users and readers. Blogger is one of the easiest ways to start a podcast fast and at no cost, so I think this tip is worth mentioning.

Blogger let's you choose whether or not to include your blog in their listings. You should make sure this is set to *Yes*. Log in to your Blogger account and choose the name of the podcast you want to configure. Click on the *Settings* tab and then the *Basic* link. Find *Add your Blog to our listings* and set it to *Yes*.

This allows you to be placed in Blogger's Recently Updated list, the rotation of blogs in the "next blog navigation bar" and a few other places. This trick just provides more visibility for free, so... flaunt it, baby.

SUMMARY

Most podcasts are published with a blog. There are numerous directories for blogs that you can submit your podcast to and get more traffic and exposure. In addition, this creates links pointing to your web site, which increases your chances of high ranking, in search engines. Use the same principles from the chapter on podcast directories for creating your title, description and keywords.

There are also a number of web sites, such as Podscope.com and SingingFish.com, that index audio on the web. These are also excellent places to submit your web site for listing.

Each time you post a new podcast episode, you should post an entry with show notes to your blog. Your blog software should be able to ping (notify) blog post listing services to have your new episode included on their sites. If you are not able to do this with your blog software, then you can also do it by hand at pingomatic.com.

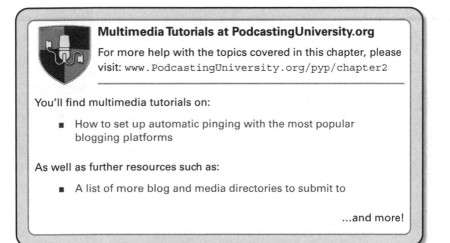

Multimedia Tutorials at PodcastingUniversity.org

For more help with the topics covered in this chapter, please visit: www.PodcastingUniversity.org/pyp/chapter2

You'll find multimedia tutorials on:

■ How to set up automatic pinging with the most popular blogging platforms

As well as further resources such as:

■ A list of more blog and media directories to submit to

...and more!

Using Blog Comments & Forum Posts to Attract New Listeners

PARTICIPATE IN THE WORLD'S LARGEST CONVERSATION

By starting a podcast, you've plugged into a large network of social media comprised of written word, recorded voice and other creations for the masses. Weblogs have exploded on the Internet, closely followed by podcasts, as participants worldwide post information, opinion, commentary, news and whatever else is on their mind. The web is turning into the world's largest conversation, and one of the voices is yours.

Your podcast has joined countless weblogs and message boards (also called discussion forums) in providing a hub of communication for people who have a common interest.

SIDENOTE: Message boards are web sites that allow users to carry on discussions by posting comments and replying to posts from others.

The fluid, immediate and social nature of blogging, podcasting and posting to forums makes it easy and fun to communicate on the web. Droves of people are getting involved. It's a social media revolution and you need to plug in.

Give them a taste of what you've got. Command some attention and turn them into loyal listeners.

You need to go where people who are interested in your topic are hanging out online. Give them a taste of what you've got. Command some attention and turn them into loyal listeners.

Whatever your podcast's topic, chances are there are weblogs and forums dedicated to it, as well. Get involved in these communities. Blogs and forums are great places for you to find loyal listeners. People who participate in blogs and forums are often rabid about the topic being discussed.

In this chapter, we'll talk about how to use blog and forum comments to attract these people to your podcast. The idea is to get your podcast's web address in front of them. Most forums and blogs let you include a link when you comment. This is usually done in the signature. Always include a link to your podcast in the signature. However, you must go about it the right way for it to work.

MESSAGE BOARD POSTS SHOULD ATTRACT LISTENERS, NOT THE FURY OF THE FORUM FLAMERS

v. flame. Internet Slang. To make insulting remarks on an Internet message board to provoke anger.

Don't just show up to a forum or blog and leave a comment like, "Hey everyone, come and check out my podcast at www.blahblahblah.com! It's swell!" This won't go over well. You'll get a few choice words in response to a post like that.

First, contribute something worthwhile to the community. Form an intelligent comment that adds to the conversation. The idea is to give people a taste of what you have to say, so they'll want to get more. When you've got them hooked, they'll notice you have a link in your signature where they can get more of what you have. This is a soft-sell technique, but it can be very powerful.

Don't just commit "drive-by posting." I know; the alternatives take more time. You're just itching to tell the world about your greatness.

But unless you want to personally learn the meaning of "flamed," then I suggest you go about this the right away.

Set a goal and plug away at it on a regular basis. It doesn't have to take much of your time. I've had great results from even minimal participation in blogs and forums. I just give it some thought and post something of value to the readers.

You'll get the feel for it. Just do it. Here are some tips for posting in discussion forums:

- Check the forum's link policy. Some prevent any linking whatsoever (hence, they're a waste of your time); some allow linking after you have posted a certain number of times; and some allow links only in your signature. Follow the rules.
- Don't submit short responses, like "thank you" or "I agree," just as an excuse to post your link.
- Don't strain your voice by posting in ALL CAPS. It's hard to read and tends to annoy.
- Keep your posts short and to the point. Use short paragraphs. One of my pet peeves is the unending paragraph. No one wants to read that. You have an *Enter* key. Use it.
- If you start a new post, use a meaningful title that will make someone want to read it. Don't just call it "Question" or "Something really cool." Be descriptive and use keywords.
- When answering a question, don't just say, "Hey! I talk about this in my podcast. Check it out." Offer some information and give a teaser of your opinion to entice people. Then link to your podcast.

If you've registered as a user of the forum, you should be able to log in and look at your user settings or profile. This is where you can enter a forum signature that will appear at the bottom of each of your posts. Look for a box or field labeled signature in your profile.

A signature is usually one to four lines long. Check forum rules for signatures. Some people just put their name in their signature. Some put their favorite quote. The best use of a signature is to promote your podcast or your web site.

Here are some tips for writing your forum signature:

- Include a link to your podcast (this should go without saying).
- Make it a headline for your podcast. Hopefully the podcast title itself is gripping.
- Draw from the description you wrote for the directories.
- Give people a reason to click through to your site and listen.
- Don't make it too long. It's a signature, not a bio.
- Only promote and link to one site. Don't try to cram your signature with your podcast link and your blog link and your MySpace link and your... you get the point. Someone is more likely to click if you give them one choice.
- Don't create a huge signature with a big image. Forum readers resent this.
- If you're on a message board where people don't know what podcasting is, then you'd better tell them in one brief statement. Notice in the figure above how I included the phrase "Listen at your leisure. It's like radio for your iPod." This gives them an idea of what a podcast is.
- If you think the forum readers will know what to do with it, you can try including your feed address in the signature, too. You can try a call to action, such as "Plug this address into your favorite feed reader: `http://www.mysite.com/feed`."

To include a link in your signature, you'll need to use a little HTML code. This is the programming language that creates the layout of most web sites. Don't worry. I won't "geek out" on you too much with HTML. I'll just show you the basics you'll need to write a forum signature with a link in it.

Here's an example of a forum signature with a link written in HTML code:

The brackets `<>` surround what are called HTML tags. The anchor tag tells the browser that this is the start of a link. The following is an example of an anchor tag that starts a link to my site, The Podcasting Underground.

```
<a href="http://www.podcastingunderground.com">
```

The `href="http://www.podcastingunderground.com"` is an element that
specifies the address that the link leads to. The `</a>` tag ends the link.
Everything in between the two tags is the text for the link. In this case
the link says Podcasting Underground. Here's the entire code for a link
to Podcasting Underground:

```
<a href="http://www.podcastingunderground.com">Podcasting
Underground</a>
```

Notice in the image I also include a tagline after the link, "News and
tips to help you succeed in podcasting. Hosted by podcasting
consultant Jason Van Orden."

This image shows how the signature would appear in the forum.

Some forums do not use HTML
to do links. Instead they use code
just for message boards called BB
Code. It's similar to HTML. Here's
how the same signature would be
written with BB Code:

```
[url=http://www.podcastingunderground.com/]Podcasting
Underground[/url]
News and tips to help you succeed in podcasting.
Hosted by podcasting consultant Jason Van Orden.
```

BB Code uses square brackets instead of angled brackets. Also, links are
created with the `[url]` tag instead of the `<a>` tag, and `href=` is not used
to specify the link. Instead, you just use `[url=http://`
`www.yourlink.com/]` to indicate the link address. The text for the link
comes right after that. Then you end the link with the `[/url]` tag.
Make sure there are no spaces or carriage returns between the `[url]` tag
at the beginning of the link and the `[/url]` tag at the end, or the link
will not display correctly. It needs to be one continuous, line even if it
wraps around in the text box when you enter it.

Here are templates for you to use to create your signature in HTML or
BB Code:

HTML

```
<a href="http://www.YourSite.com">Your Podcast Title</a>
A brief, catchy description or tagline goes here.
```

BB CODE

```
[url=http://www.YourSite.com/]Your Podcast Title[/url]
A brief, catchy description or tagline goes here.
```

If you want other ideas of how podcasters use their forum signatures,
visit the boards at www.podcastalley.com or www.podcastpickle.com.
These are communities for podcasters. This is a great place to start
posting, because people on these sites already like listening to podcasts.
Eventually, though, you'll need to promote yourself outside of
podcasting circles.

OTHER CREATIVE FORUM PROMOTION IDEAS

Another way to promote your podcast in discussion forums is with your
avatar. An avatar is the little image that usually appears to the left of
your post. Often people use some goofy looking caricature or annoying
animated clipart of a smiley with an attitude problem.

If you've created a square podcast logo for your show, you could also use
it as your avatar. This will capture people's attention and help brand
your show, as it appears next to each of your posts. It's best to include
your web address in the graphic, but only if it will be readable.

Here is an example of a podcast logo that could be
used as an avatar. It's readable and contains the web
address. You need to make sure that the graphic is
not too large when it appears in the forum. Many
forum moderators and participants look down on,
or even forbid, large avatars. An image that is 150 x
150 pixels is probably the limit.

Here's another example of an avatar that even manages to fit in a tagline to tell you what the podcast is about.

You should be able to change your avatar, in your forum profile. Most forums let you use a custom avatar by either uploading an image or by entering a web address to a file.

Feedburner.com offers a great feature called the Headline Animator. This is often used in forum signatures as well. The Headline Animator is a graphic that scrolls through the titles of the last few episodes in your feed. It also contains the name of your podcast or another headline if you wish to customize it.

FeedBurner offers two different looks for your Headline Animator—classic and email signature. The former is their original box that works well on web sites. The latter is a simpler format specifically for email and forum signatures.

The Headline Animator works best if the titles of your episodes will grab people's interest and make them want to click. You need a strong headline and alluring episode titles to rotate in the image, in order to pique someone's curiosity. If you name your episodes just *Episode #X*, it won't be effective. However, you're likely to get some clicks if you're posting in an investing forum and your animator displays an episode titled *Why Some People Almost Always Make Money in the Stock Market*.

It's not a bad idea to include a link to your site beneath the animator as well. It might not be clear to everyone that they can click the image as a link.

You must be a FeedBurner user to create a Headline Animator. You can create a Headline Animator from inside your FeedBurner account. Here's how to create one for your podcast:

1. Log in to your FeedBurner account.
2. Click on the name of the podcast for which you want to create the Headline Animator.
3. Click the *Publicize* tab.
4. Click the *Headline Animator* button.
5. Next to *Select an Animator style,* choose the classic or email signature animator. For forums, I suggest using the email signature style.
6. Next to *Update the Animator Title,* enter your headline or simply the title of your podcast.

Your Active Animator Selection

Feb 28, 2006
Ep10: Common Fears of Going into Biz on
from **Internet Business Mastery**
Subscribe now

Copy this HTML code for use in your email program:

```
<a href="http://feeds.feedburner.com/ibm"><img
src="http://feeds.feedburner.com/ibm.gif" style="border:0" alt="Internet
Business Mastery"/></a>
```

View a Tech Tip for successfully incorporating this signature code into popular email applications like Outlook/Outlook Express, Thunderbird, and Yahoo! Mail, plus a workaround for GMail.

Animator Settings

Select an Animator style: [Email Signature Animator]

Update the Animator Title: [Internet Business Mastery]

Save This service is active   Deactivate

FeedBurner will generate HTML code for you. Some of the same HTML tags from earlier are in this code as well. Here's an example of the classic Headline Animator code for my podcast, *Internet Business Mastery*:

```
<a href=http://www.internet-based-business-mastery.com>
<img src="http://feeds.feedburner.com/ibm.gif" height="67"
width="200" style="border:0" alt="Internet Business Mastery
Podcast"/>
</a>
```

This example is for a classic email signature Headline Animator which links to the *Internet Business Mastery* web site by default. To modify what the Headline Animator links to, change the web

address that appears in quotes after `href=`. You can change this to your link address, if you prefer. If you use the email signature format, the link will be set to your feed by default.

The FeedBurner code also contains an `<img>` tag to place the Headline Animator image. The image tag starts with `<img>` and contains a source element (`src=`). This indicates the location of the image. In this case, it's `src=http://feeds.feedburner.com/ibm.gif` which points to my headline image on FeedBurner's site.

There are a few other elements in the <img> tag that you don't need to worry about. Notice that the image tag is standalone, meaning that there's no closing tag for it. All the needed info is contained in the one tag.

You can just copy and paste the code from FeedBurner into your signature if the message board accepts HTML. If the forum only accepts BB Code, then you'll need to tweak things a bit.

Here's what the previous example would look like if written with BB Code:

```
[url=http://www.internet-based-business-mastery.com]
[img]http://feeds.feedburner.com/ibm.gif[/img] [/url]
```

One main difference in BB Code from HTML is that it does have an opening image tag `[img]` and a closing tag image tag `[/img]`.

COMMENTING ON BLOGS TO GET LINKS AND LISTENERS

Most blog posts allow readers to post a comment to give feedback, ask questions or make suggestions based on the blogger's entry. This is a great place to jump in, be heard and get your link in front of potential listeners. If your comments are interesting, people will click through to your podcast.

This is very similar to forum posting. The same tips apply here. Don't indulge in drive-by commenting. Add something of value to the conversation. Check the bloggers policy on comments. Make sure you're allowed to include a link. Most blogs allow you to enter a web address that will be linked to along with your name.

Don't indulge in drive-by commenting. Add something of value to the conversation.

POST A COMMENT
Are you aware of our Comment Policy?
Name:
Jason

Email Address:
email@domain.com

URL:
http://www.podcastingunderground.c ☐ Remember personal info?

Comments: (you may use HTML tags for style*)
My commment goes here.

Jason
<a href=http://www.PodcastingUnderground.com>Podcasting Underground</a>

Post

Preview
*Tags allowed: a href, b, i, br/, p, strong, em, ul, ol, li, blockquote, p

Sometimes, you can also use HTML code for a link in the comment box. Usually the blog will indicate if HTML is allowed or not. Some blogs don't permit it to cut down on comment spam. Here's an example of a blog comment form with an HTML code link in the comment box.

ZEROING IN ON THE LOW HANGING FRUIT:
HOW TO FIND NICHE-TARGETED BLOGS AND FORUMS TO POST TO

I have a few strategies that I use to find blogs and forums to post to. The first place you should look is in a search engine such as Google. You can search for *"your topic" forum* (substitute your topic with the subject of your podcast). This should give you a list of search results that link to a forum related to your topic.

Try the search with and without quotes around your topic phrase. This will probably produce two different sets of search results. You can also try it with and without plurals. For example, if you have a podcast about dog care, you'd do the following searches:

1. "dog care" forum
2. dog care forum
3. "dog care" forums
4. dog care forums

You can also try different variations on your topic phrase. If you talk about baseball equipment in your podcast, you could search for both *"baseball equipment" forum* and *"baseball gear" forum*, not to mention you may want to try just *baseball forum*.

To find forums to post to for *Internet Business Mastery*, I'd search for the following phrases in Google, with and without quotes around the topic phrase:

- Internet business forum
- Internet marketing forum
- online marketing forum
- online business forum
- entrepreneur forum
- small business forum

Be creative. Spend time conducting thorough searches, with a variety of keywords. The goal is to find forums that are as targeted as possible to your podcast's subject. The more targeted and relevant the site, the more response you'll get.

Read through the first page of results for each search. Click any of the results that look promising. If you find a forum that appears to be frequented by the kind of people who would like your podcast, register for a username on the forum, bookmark the site, change your signature and avatar in your profile and return regularly to post.

Technorati (www.technorati.com) is a great tool for finding well-trafficked blogs related to your topic. Technorati visits millions of blogs every day to index what people are blogging about. They feature two different sections to look in. You can search under the *Search* tab as well as the *Tag* tab. The results are based on two different systems of cataloging blog topics and posts. I'll explain more about this in the chapter on using Technorati tags.

When you search for your podcast's subject in Technorati, you'll obtain a list of the most recent blog entries on that topic. The search results contain the post's title, how long ago it was posted, the blog's web address and a snippet of the blog entry. Scan the results for something that looks interesting that you can comment on. Click the post title to be taken to the web page for that blog entry.

Here are some search results for Internet marketing:

Episode #11: Finally, the Listener Comment show!

By Sterling & Jay in Internet Business Mastery: The... 7 days ago

Episode #11: Finally, the Listern Comment show! Categories: Podcast Click Here to Download and Listen Now: [Download This Episode] As Promised! ... Comment' show and other questions as an entire **internet business** mastery 'topic' show. As always ... **business, internet business**, ebay tips, entrepreneur, e-myth, entrepreneurship, eBay secrets

Make money working from home

In Make Money Online Links 7 days ago

Make money working from home ... This Site Gives You the Tools to Make Money Online. (PRWEB) ... Make money online.Start

I try to sift through the results to find the blogs that get the most traffic - i.e., the blogs that have more visitors who will see my comment and link. To find the most popular blogs, hover your mouse pointer over the little icon right under the post title that looks like a speech bubble from the Sunday comics. It's the second icon from the left.

When you hover your mouse pointer over this icon, there will be a little pop up that states how many links Technorati has tracked to this blog from other weblogs. The more links to the post, the more traffic it's likely to get, making it a better candidate for your comments. If you find a blog that you like to comment on that brings you traffic, bookmark it and return to comment regularly.

Another good tool to find blogs on your podcast's topic is Google Blog Search (blogsearch.google.com). This engine also returns blog posts on a given topic. You can sort the results by relevance or by date. Above the blog post results, Google gives you a list of blogs that it deems to be the most related to the topic. If a blog is listed here, it probably has a lot of links to it and is worth checking out for commenting.

I suggest being creative and thorough in searching for related blog posts. Going back to the example of a podcast on dog care (even though I'm not a pet person), I'd search for the following phrases in Technorati and Google Blog Search to find related blogs:

- dog care
- dog training
- dog grooming
- caring for dogs
- dog health

When you find a good blog that is related to your podcast's subject, bookmark the site. You can even subscribe to its feed to get notification of all the new posts to that blog.

Set a goal to post to blogs and forums a certain number of times each week. If you make regular efforts to get the word out and get your link in front of people, you'll draw more listeners to your podcast. Also, frequently look for new forums and blogs. If you settle into posting to the same ones, the results will level off, because many of the readers will have already seen your link.

The other benefit of posting to forums and blogs is that it scatters links to your podcast all over the Internet. Search engines love to slurp up these links as they crawl through the web. More links to your podcast leads to higher rankings in the search engines.

SUMMARY

Your podcast is part of a global conversation that permeates weblogs, message boards and other social web sites. You can attract loyal listeners who are passionate about your topic by participating in these social networks.

Find blogs and discussion forums that focus on your podcast's topic using Technorati and Google. Avoid making comments that come across as a blatant promotion. Offer valuable insights when you post. Always include a tagline and link to your podcast in the signature of your post or comment. If what you have to say resonates with people, they'll click through to your site and listen.

Multimedia Tutorials at PodcastingUniversity.org

For more help with the topics covered in this chapter, please visit: www.PodcastingUniversity.org/pyp/chapter3

You'll find multimedia tutorials on:

- Creating forum signatures with HTML and/or BBCode
- Creating a Headline Animator in FeedBurner
- Using FeedBurner's Headline Animator in your forum posts
- Using HTML links in blog comments and forum posts
- Finding good blogs and forums for promoting your podcast

...and more!

Free, Targeted Visitors—
Can You Ask for Anything More?

VYING FOR THE TOP

Clicks from search engine results pages are one of the most sought after sources of traffic on the Internet. This traffic is free and tends to produce well-targeted visitors. There's a good chance that someone who clicks to your site from Google wants something that you have. This is called organic search traffic to distinguish it from paid search listings, such as the ones that appear on the right side of Google's search results.

It takes time, patience and careful planning to get organic search engine traffic, but it can turn into a virtual floodgate of listeners if you play the game right. You need to start now, to reap the benefits later. Your success will vary depending on how much time you dedicate to getting search traffic, the topic of your podcast, how often people search for your kind of content and how many other pages are competing to be listed for the same search phrases.

The three top dogs in the search engine world are Google, Yahoo and MSN. According to SearchEngineWatch.com, Google gets 46.3% of online searches, Yahoo gets 23.4% and MSN gets 11.4%. As you can see, if you concentrate on getting listed in these three, you'll hit the majority of searches performed on the web.

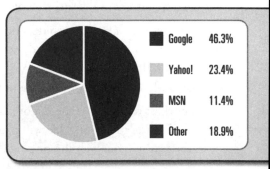

Google	46.3%
Yahoo!	23.4%
MSN	11.4%
Other	18.9%

In addition, most search traffic comes from the first page of search results. The top three slots get the vast majority of clicks.

The goal of search engines is to serve up the most relevant information when someone searches for a given phrase. The engines give top search placement to web pages that they think offer the searcher what she's looking for.

Your goal is to get ranked as high as possible in search results for phrases that are relevant to your podcast's topic.

Your goal is to get ranked as high as possible in search results for phrases that are relevant to your podcast's topic. To get one of the top positions you need to provide content that the search engines see as on topic and good in quality.

The obvious first step is to create and post good content to your site on a regular basis. In addition, we'll talk about a number of other things that you can do to make your pages more appealing to the search engines and land higher rankings. First, let's take a look at how the search engines find your web page.

ROBOTS HARVESTING AND SPIDERS CRAWLING

Cataloging the information superhighway is a gigantic task. The only way search engines can keep up with the amount of data coming and going on the Internet is by using an array of computer programs referred to affectionately as spiders or robots. These programs are designed to automatically surf sites and store what they find.

This process is referred to as spiders harvesting or crawling web sites. Sounds like a B-grade sci-fi flick, doesn't it? The search engine spiders constantly follow links and jump from page to page, looking for changes and new content to include in search engine results.

It's important to note that the major search engines' spiders do not crawl and index audio yet. This will probably eventually change. For now, the text on your web site or blog determines how search engines list your web pages. It's important to provide good show notes not only for your listeners, but also for the search engines.

Moreover, you can provide additional text content on your site that relates to the topic of your podcast. I'm not saying to neglect your audio. After all, there's a reason you're a podcaster. Just consider adding some additional text content or blog entries to your site. This content will show up in the search engines and attract potential listeners to your podcast. You need to give search engines what they're looking for—quality text content.

The engines use several factors to automatically determine the subject matter and quality of a web page. Their exact formulas are constantly changing, not to mention they're guarded as carefully as the formula for Coca-Cola.

However, experience and research have revealed many time-tested techniques for improving a web page's ranking in the search engines. This involves adding posts and pages to your blog or site that are written and designed to increase their ranking for a given search phrase. This is called search engine optimization (SEO). But before you can optimize pages on your site, you need to know what phrases to target.

KEYWORDS ARE KING

Search engine optimization is based on keywords. These are the phrases that people who are interested in content such as yours are likely to search for. We already talked about the importance of using keywords in your podcast title and description in the podcast directories. Now we'll look at how to use keywords on your web site or blog to attract search engine traffic.

Your search engine marketing strategy begins with creating a list of words and phrases for which potential listeners are likely to search. Then, research which ones are the most popular and the easiest to compete for. Finally, you will prioritize your list and choose the best keywords.

Start your list by stepping into your potential listeners' shoes. What phrases might they search for to find content on your topic? I suggest entering the phrases down a column in a spreadsheet. This will make it easier for you to later analyze and prioritize them. Brainstorm with friends or colleagues who are familiar with the subject. Just write down anything that comes to mind. You can edit the list later.

Keep in mind that phrases that are two to four words long are better. Research shows that people who search for longer phrases have a better idea as to what they're looking for and are more likely to take action. You'll get better results from targeting longer phrases. This is easiest if your podcast is about a niche topic. If your topic is too broad or if you try to be all things to all people, you'll have a tough time pinpointing keywords that convey a good ranking.

Imagine trying to get a top listing for the word *air*. Maybe you talk about air quality and air purifiers. First of all, if you have a podcast on air quality, more power to you. I guess you really can start a podcast about anything. Second, because *air* is a very broad term, you would be competing with dozens of other unrelated topics such as air travel. It would be better to target longer phrases like *air purifier reviews, air purification* or *indoor air quality*. The more words in a phrase, the easier it will be to get a good ranking for it.

Let's look at an example. We'll brainstorm a list of keyword phrases for a podcast on baseball equipment. The first step is to think of what phrases a potential listener would search to find content about baseball equipment. These initially come to mind:

- baseball equipment
- baseball gear
- baseball gloves
- baseball bats
- protective baseball gear
- baseball shoes
- baseball hats

Notice how I left the word baseball by itself off of this list. Even though it's a relevant word, it's too broad. It will be difficult to compete for a high ranking for that word alone.

This list is a decent start, but there are probably many phrases we're overlooking. These three tips can help you expand your keyword list:

1. **Use Online Keyword Tools**

   Several keyword tools on the Internet take a phrase and then return other common search terms related to it. Here are some tools that I suggest:

   - Nichebot
     `www.nichebot.com`

   - Overture Keyword Tool
     `inventory.overture.com`

   - Google Adwords Keyword Tool
     `adwords.google.com/select/KeywordToolExternal`

Keyword Variations	Site-Related Keywords

   Enter one keyword or phrase per line:

   ```
   internet business
   internet marketing
   ```
   ☑ Use synonyms

   [Get More Keywords]

   Show columns: Upda

   More specific keywords - sorted by relevance [?]

   Keywords

   internet business

   internet marketing

   internet business for sale

   turnkey internet business

   business internet connection

   top internet business

   internet marketing jobs

2. **Take a Look at the Top 10 Results in Google, MSN and Search**

   Search for phrases you've already listed and visit the sites that show up in the top 10 results. Take note of other relevant phrases that you find on their pages.

3. Look at Your Site Statistics

If you already have a web site or blog, look at your site statistics. Most statistics show some information on what search phrases are currently bringing traffic to your site. Add these to your list.

Search Keyphrases (Top 10) Full list	
42 different keyphrases	Search
baseball podcast	97
baseball gear	75
baseball equipment	56
baseball gear reviews	40
baseball gear podcast	33
baseball jerseys	20

To expand our list of phrases for the baseball equipment podcast, we first turn to Nichebot. Entering the phrase *baseball equipment* into this tool returns more phrases such as *discount baseball equipment, youth baseball equipment, Easton baseball equipment* and more. We also can enter in *baseball gear* and the other phrases we had already chosen. Then we turn to the Google and Overture keyword tools to see if there are any other phrases we missed.

I usually continue this process until I have at least 50 phrases. You may even come up with a few hundred. For simplicity, we'll stop with the 20 in this example. Here's the list now:

baseball equipment

baseball gear

baseball gloves

baseball bats

protective baseball gear

baseball shoes

baseball hats

discount baseball equipment

youth baseball equipment

easton baseball equipment

rawlings baseball equipment

baseball training equipment

baseball protective equipment

baseball fan gear

baseball catchers gear

baseball umpire gear

wood baseball bats

wooden baseball bats

custom baseball gloves

baseball jerseys

When you make your own list, remember to use synonyms. For example, when making a list for *Internet Business Mastery,* we used the phrases *online business* and *web business* in addition to *Internet business.* Above, we used the word *equipment* as well as *gear.*

Finally, go through the list and delete any phrases that don't really pertain to the topic of your podcast. You don't want to make people mad by luring them to your web site looking for something you don't offer. In our example, the phrases all seem to be relevant to our topic.

Here's one more thought. Not only do we now have the start of a great search engine marketing plan, we also have a list of ideas for future episodes of our baseball gear podcast.

NOT ALL KEYWORDS ARE CREATED EQUAL: KEYWORD RESEARCH AND PRIORITIZATION

It's important to prioritize your keywords so you can concentrate your efforts on those that are most likely to bring you traffic. This is a simple question of supply and demand. Work on getting traffic from keyword phrases that get the most searches but don't have so much competition that it will be hard to stand out, or get high rankings for them.

It's important to prioritize your keywords so you can concentrate your efforts on those that are most likely to bring you traffic.

To analyze this I like to create a spreadsheet. I put the keywords in the first column and then label the second and third columns *Searches* and *Competition.*

The major search engines don't release the number of searches they get for phrases. Fortunately, there are tools that have ways of estimating this for us. It's important to use tools to measure the popularity of search phrases. If I just assume that one phrase is more popular, I often find out later that I was wrong. The tool I rely on most often for this information is Nichebot.

When you search for a phrase at Nichebot, you'll notice that not only does it return other similar phrases, but it also gives a number called

Count for each of them. I won't go into how this number is derived or what exactly it means. It's sufficient to know that the higher the number, the more the phrase gets searched. Put this number in the *Searches* column of your spreadsheet for each keyword phrase. If you have phrases that you picked up from Google or Overture's suggestions tools, you'll need to enter them into Nichebot to get their count.

Here's what the spreadsheet would look like for our example keyword list:

Keyword Phrase	Searches
baseball equipment	359,969
baseball gear	37,997
baseball gloves	341,475
baseball bats	469,953
protective baseball gear	732
baseball shoes	25,193
baseball hats	148,505
discount baseball equipment	9,409
youth baseball equipment	5,657
easton baseball equipment	4,723
rawlings baseball equipment	2,860
baseball training equipment	2,550
baseball protective equipment	2,436
baseball fan gear	374
baseball catchers gear	523
baseball umpire gear	466
wood baseball bats	12,862
wooden baseball bats	3,629
custom baseball gloves	2,770
baseball jerseys	59,210

Next, measure the competition level for each phrase. There are a few ways to do this. The easiest is to enter the search phrase and take a look in the upper right-hand corner at the number of results that are indicated. You'll see something like "Results 1 - 10 of about 2,000,000". The last number is an estimate of how many pages Google has indexed for that search phrase. This also is the number that Nichebot returns in the *Competition* column.

Many search engine marketers use this number to measure the competition for getting ranked for a given phrase. The more pages indexed for a phrase, the harder it will be to get a high ranking yourself. I find this method to be too simplistic.

I prefer an analysis that is not only based on the number of pages listed for a phrase, but also the quality of those pages.

Enter the following search in Google: *allintitle:"insert phrase here"* (insert your keyword phrase with the quotes around it). The allintitle search returns only pages that have the exact search phrase in their page title. The page title is what appears in the title bar at the top of your browser window. Look in the upper right-hand corner of the Google search results to see how many pages use the phrase in their title.

There's a reason why this number is a better measurement of the competition for a phrase. A web pages' title is one of the many things Google looks at to determine if the page is relevant to a search term. If a web page has a search phrase in its title, it will get a higher ranking for that search. Counting these pages is a better indication of the competition for a phrase. Perform the allintitle search for each of your keywords and record the number of results for each keyword in a column of your spreadsheet labeled *Competition.*

Now find the best keywords by weighing the number of searches against the competition. You want to concentrate on the most popular words that don't have too much competition. You'll calculate a rating for each keyword to help you do this. Calculating the rating is easy, especially if you've been using spreadsheet software, such as Excel, to build your keyword list. Name the third column of your spreadsheet *Rating*. This is the formula for keyword rating:

Rating = (Searches x Searches)/Competition

Set up your spreadsheet to calculate the rating in the fourth column for each of your keywords. Then sort the keyword list by the rating, starting with the highest rating down to the lowest:

Keyword Phrase	Searches	Competition	Rating
baseball gear	37,997	662	2,180,924
baseball gloves	341,475	56,100	2,078,524
baseball bats	469,953	174,000	1,269,286
baseball hats	148,505	18,400	1,198,573
baseball shoes	25,193	858	739,729
baseball equipment	359,969	239,000	542,166
wood baseball bats	12,862	1,180	140,196
discount baseball equipment	9,409	920	96,227
youth baseball equipment	5,657	449	71,273
baseball jerseys	59,210	63,900	54,864
wooden baseball bats	3,629	377	34,933
easton baseball equipment	4,723	713	31,286
custom baseball gloves	2,770	289	26,550
baseball training equipment	2,550	465	13,984
rawlings baseball equipment	2,860	765	10,692
protective baseball gear	732	54	9,923
baseball catchers gear	523	70	3,908
baseball protective equipment	2,436	2,480	2,393
baseball umpire gear	466	97	2,239
baseball fan gear	374	10,800	13

The keywords at the top are the ones you want to use first. Take the top 10-15 for now. We'll call these your primary keywords. These are the words that have the best potential of generating traffic. After you've optimized pages for the top 10-15 keywords, you can take another set of words from your list.

SEARCH ENGINE OPTIMIZATION

Now that you have a list of keyword phrases, I'll take you through a simple crash course in the art and science of using them to optimize your web pages for search engines. I'll show you basic techniques for getting higher search engine rankings for your primary keywords. The goal is to have at least one optimized page that ranks well for each of your primary keywords. This page will attract potential listeners to your podcast when they search for the phrase and click through to your site.

Before we move on, I should emphasize that, first and foremost, you must provide quality content. Search engine optimization is not about tricking Google into giving your site higher rankings. Many shady techniques come and go that fool search engines into giving undeserving pages top search positions. The effects are short-lived and get sites banned in the end.

Search engines need to provide quality results to their users. They will do what they must to preserve their integrity. Concentrate first on providing good content in your podcast, and on your site, and you'll achieve long-lasting search engine success.

A successful search engine optimization strategy consists of two parts:

- **On-page optimization** involves using one or two search phrases on a web page in such a way that the search engine sees that page as highly relevant when the phrase is searched. It takes time to build up quality content and get it noticed by the search engines. You must consistently work at it.
- **Off-page optimization** involves getting other sites on the topic to link to the page. The more inbound links on a web page, the more authority and popularity the search engines think it has. This also takes some time, because search engines like pages that have gained inbound links gradually and naturally. When a site gains tons of inbound links all at once, it's a sign that something isn't kosher and search engines look askance on this.

ON-PAGE OPTIMIZATION: DESIGNING WEB PAGES THAT ATTRACT THE MOST SEARCH TRAFFIC

There are a multitude of factors a search engine examines on a web page to decide how to rank it. The content on an optimized web page or blog post is focused on one main topic and uses one or two primary keywords throughout the page, or in certain places on the page. To determine the topic and quality of your content, the engine looks at the text to see what phrases are used most, how they are used and where they appear on the page.

Here are some places where it's important to include primary keywords to optimize a page for those phrases:

1. **Blog Post Title**
   If the page is a post to your blog, use the phrase in the title of the post. The post might be either an episode of your podcast or just an additional article that you write and post. If it's just a regular web page on your site, then use the phrase in the heading for that page. If possible, you want your keyword phrase to be the first thing that the search engine spider sees on your site. Spiders crawl web pages from top to bottom.

2. **First Paragraph**
   Use the phrase at least once in the first paragraph. If you are optimizing show notes, use the phrase in the first line or bullet point.

3. **Throughout the Text**
   If a phrase appears more often than other words on the page, it makes it easy for the search engines to determine the topic of the content. But don't go overboard. To get the right balance, search engine marketers measure how many times a keyword phrase appears in the text relative to the total word count of the page. This is called keyword density.

   For example, let's say you have a post that is 500 words long and you use a three-word phrase 10 times in the post. In this case, 30 of the 500 words are keywords. Thirty is six percent of 500, so the keyword density is six percent. A keyword density of 3-7% is a good balance.

   You also want to make sure the content is still readable and makes sense to your site visitors. If you use the phrase too much, this is called keyword stuffing and it can get your site banned. I would stay under 10% to remain on the safe side.

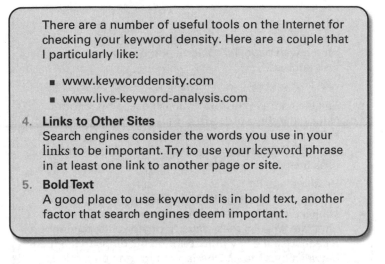

There are a number of useful tools on the Internet for checking your keyword density. Here are a couple that I particularly like:

- www.keyworddensity.com
- www.live-keyword-analysis.com

4. **Links to Other Sites**
   Search engines consider the words you use in your links to be important. Try to use your keyword phrase in at least one link to another page or site.

5. **Bold Text**
   A good place to use keywords is in bold text, another factor that search engines deem important.

These are a few of the easiest ways to optimize a page for a given phrase. I have listed a few more tips below, but they require a little more technical understanding of page design. If you're not familiar with how to edit these things, just skip them or get a web designer to help you. Each of the following is another place that the search engine looks to determine how to rank the web page:

1. **Title Tag for the Web Page** (`<title>`)
   Behind the scenes, in the HTML code, there is a `<title>` tag. This tag tells the browser the name of a web page. This is what is displayed in the bar at the top of the browser window. This is different than the title or heading for a blog post, although some blog software uses the blog post title in the web page title. If the search engines see your keyword phrase in the page title, the page will get a higher ranking. Some blogs use the title of the blog post in the title tag for the web page.

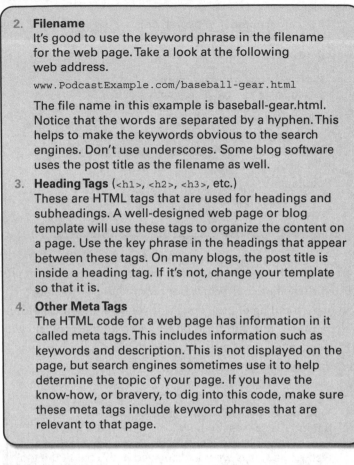

2. **Filename**
   It's good to use the keyword phrase in the filename for the web page. Take a look at the following web address.

   `www.PodcastExample.com/baseball-gear.html`

   The file name in this example is baseball-gear.html. Notice that the words are separated by a hyphen. This helps to make the keywords obvious to the search engines. Don't use underscores. Some blog software uses the post title as the filename as well.

3. **Heading Tags** (`<h1>`, `<h2>`, `<h3>`, etc.)
   These are HTML tags that are used for headings and subheadings. A well-designed web page or blog template will use these tags to organize the content on a page. Use the key phrase in the headings that appear between these tags. On many blogs, the post title is inside a heading tag. If it's not, change your template so that it is.

4. **Other Meta Tags**
   The HTML code for a web page has information in it called meta tags. This includes information such as keywords and description. This is not displayed on the page, but search engines sometimes use it to help determine the topic of your page. If you have the know-how, or bravery, to dig into this code, make sure these meta tags include keyword phrases that are relevant to that page.

OFF-PAGE OPTIMIZATION: GETTING LINKS TO YOUR WEB PAGES

Search engines have learned that they can tell the quality and popularity of a web page by looking at the number and quality of the links to it from other sites. Higher ranked pages tend to have the following:

- Inbound links from other authoritative and popular web pages with content on the same topic. A link from a site like Yahoo or About.com will be considered a lot more valuable than a link from a little-known blog.
- A lot of inbound links have built up naturally over time. This is a sign that a page has quality content and people are taking notice.

- Inbound links that contain the keyword phrase in the link text (anchor text). For example, a page on baseball gear will get ranked higher if there are a lot of links pointing to it that have *baseball gear* in the link text.

In an ideal world, your pages would have lots of links from high ranking and popular sites that use the same keywords in their link text. Of course, you usually can't control the inbound links you get, but here are several strategies for getting more of them:

1. **Create Great Content**
   If your content is good, people will want to link to it. If you release insightful and entertaining information, it will attract attention.

2. **Encourage Listeners to Link**
   My *Internet Business Mastery* co-host and I realized that our listeners started linking to us in their blogs. When we see this, we give them a shout out and thank them in the show. Listeners love the attention and it encourages others to link to us as well. After all, they want their own special mention. We also let our listeners know that if they find our content useful, the best thing they can do for us is refer others to the show, especially on their own site or blog.

3. **Submit to Directories**
   Every podcast or blog directory you submit to usually results in a link back your site. There also are a number of other general web directories that you can submit to. One well-respected directory is the Open Directory Project (*dmoz.org*), screened by volunteer editors. Google even uses info from this directory in its search results.

4. **Email Webmasters and Bloggers**
   There's nothing wrong with sending a brief email asking someone to link you to his or her site. You don't want it to come across as spam or just another form email. Personalize it a bit. Show that you know something about their site and state why including a link to your site adds value to theirs. If nothing else, you can offer to exchange links. Although reciprocal links do not weigh as strongly with search engines, they're better than nothing.

5. **Post Comments to Forums and Blogs**
   In an earlier chapter, I discussed the benefits of posting to forums or blogs. I reiterate this point here, to emphasize that it usually results in a link back to your own site. Search engines see these as inbound links.

6. **Write Articles or Blog Entries for Other Sites**
   Webmasters are always looking for fresh content to post to their site. It's not always easy to create or find what they need. If you write a quality article, you should be able to find other sites or blogs that are willing to post it with your name and a link to your podcast at the end. The article only needs to be 500 or so words long.

SEO DON'TS

The following practices can get you banned from the search engines and should be avoided.

- **Overusing a Phrase on a Page**
  In the early days of search engine marketing, some webmasters would cram their web pages full of keywords to get better search results. The search engines got smart to this and will now penalize your site if they see it.

- **Using Invisible Keywords**
  What if you just cram your site with keywords, but make them white on a white background? No one will see it, right? Wrong. Search engine spiders are smarter than you might think. They will still see this and may ban your site as a result.

- **Throwing Up Links on Any Page, Even If It's Not On Topic**
  Search engines like to see lots of inbound links to your pages, but not if it means you have links from lots of random sites on topics not related to your own.

The basic idea is to not do anything meant to fool the search engines or searchers into thinking your content is on a subject it is not, or that is better than it really is. The search engines constantly update their formulas to weed out sites using so-called "black hat" optimization techniques.

SEO-FRIENDLY WEB ADDRESSES

If you're just starting your podcast and have not yet chosen a web address, it's worth giving careful consideration to choosing an address that contains your primary keywords. This gets a little tricky, because you want your web address and the name of your podcast to be the same, or at least related. The ideal situation is to choose a name for your show that uses one of your best keyword phrases, and use that as your web address, as well.

Let's go back to the baseball gear podcast example. A search engine friendly name for this podcast would be Baseball Gear Podcast, Baseball Gear Live or Baseball Gear Review. Granted, these may not be the most interesting names, but they'll get better rankings in search engines and podcast directories.

The first thing to do is to check if your desired domain is available. I do this at 000domains.com, because it has a tool for checking multiple web addresses at the same time. After I find an available address that I like, I usually register it at 1and1.com.

At this book's writing, BaseballGearReview.com is available. Remember how I mentioned that hyphens help search engines recognize your keywords? I could also use Baseball-Gear-Review.com. Which is better? It depends. For search engine traffic, the hyphenated web address is better and will give you a bit of an edge, but it's less than ideal for printed or word-of-mouth marketing. However, there's a way to get the best of both worlds.

In this case, I'd register the hyphenated web address (Baseball-Gear-Review.com) first and host my podcast blog or site at that address. When I submit to directories, build inbound links or perform any other online marketing, I'd use the web address with hyphens. This is the address that search engines pick up, because that is where the site is hosted. Then, I'd register the web address without the hyphens (BaseballGearReview.com) and tell the registrar to forward that address to the site at the hyphenated web address.

For example, if you go to InternetBusinessMastery.com, you'll be forwarded to Internet-Based-Business-Mastery.com. We use the first address when giving it on the show, by word-of-mouth and on business cards. We use the hyphenated address in all of our online marketing. We do that to get the extra edge in the search rankings for the phrase *Internet based business*, which is one of our top keyword phrases.

How much exactly does this help? I can't say for sure, but it seems to work for me time and time again. Using this strategy, I've landed sites on the first page of the Google results in a couple of months. Search engines may recognize your keywords without the hyphens, but I like to stack the odds in my favor as much as I can.

When you start a new site, I suggest linking to it from one of your other sites that is already indexed in the engines. If you don't have another web site to link from, ask another podcaster or blogger to link to your podcast on their home page. This will help the spiders find your podcast. Search engine spiders can only find new pages by following links on pages they already know about.

WEBLOGS: THE PREFERRED FOOD FOR SPIDERS

Search engines especially like blogs. Weblogs are usually updated often and have become a popular source of information. Spiders love to feed on fresh quality content. Search engines always index updates to my blogs faster than changes to my other sites. Whenever I start a new site, I link to it from one of my weblogs to help the spiders find it faster. This is another reason why I prefer to publish my podcasts with blogs.

PHRASES FROM THE PERIPHERY

I've talked a lot about finding primary keywords that have high demand without too much competition and focusing on optimizing for these phrases. This is the foundation of a solid SEO plan. But there are other words and phrases that should not go overlooked.

Any phrase that appears on your web pages could bring occasional search traffic. I always include names of all the people and places that I discuss on GothamCast. Now and again I get traffic because someone searched for information about a café I recommended on my podcast. In my Podcasting Underground show notes I include names of products, services and companies that I talk about in the show. Each of these phrases could bring in traffic when searched.

Keep an eye on your stats to see what phrases are bringing in traffic. You might get traffic from phrases that you never imagined. Occasionally, something will pop up that you hadn't expected. Try optimizing for some of these "found" phrases and see if you can't milk them for more traffic.

KEEPING AN EYE ON YOUR SEO PROGRESS

From time to time, check the rank of your site in the three major search engines for each of your major keywords. If you are moving up the charts, keep up what you're doing.

Here are a few ways to maintain your rankings and inbound links:

- Go to `gorank.com` or `digitalpoint.com/tools/keywords` to check your search engine rankings over time.
- Use `uptimebot.com` to do an analysis across all major search engines.
- Do a search directly in one of the search engines for `link:www.InsertSiteAddress.com`. Placing link: in front of a web address in a search engine will return the links that the engine has found that point to that web address. You can also do this for a specific web page on your site. Take note, Google doesn't include all of the inbound links it has found in the link: search results. The number of results returned in Google for this search will be lower than in Yahoo or MSN.
- Go to `www.pubsub.com/site_stats.php` and enter the web address to a page on your site. This will produce a report of links that have been found to that page. What's really cool about this tool is that there's an RSS feed available for any search, so you can have regular updates sent to your newsreader.

USING ADDITIONAL TEXT CONTENT WITH YOUR PODCAST

At the very least, I encourage you to apply as many of these techniques as you can to your show notes. This will make a big difference in your search engine rankings. In addition, I suggest posting additional text content to your site that has been search engine optimized.

This is as easy as writing an article that is 500-1,000 words long on each of your primary keyword phrases. Use all the on-page optimization tips listed in this chapter. Each of these pages becomes a doorway into your site that will help you climb up the search engine rankings and bring in traffic.

Another idea is to do a podcast episode around each phrase and have it transcribed. Then you can tweak it a little to optimize it and post it to your blog or site.

PATIENCE, PRACTICE AND PERSEVERANCE

It's important to put consistent effort into optimizing your site for search engines. Eventually, these SEO techniques will become second nature. Even if you don't see results right away, don't get discouraged. Some niches are just really competitive and you have to get creative to break through the competition.

Believe me, I know. Internet marketing and business is a very competitive niche, full of aggressive people who know how to perform search engine marketing. That's why I decided to start a podcast on the subject. Maybe I was motivated by the challenge, or maybe I'm just a masochist. Regardless, I continue to plug away at my SEO as a long-term marketing plan. It's an investment that pays dividends in the form of traffic.

You can move forward knowing that you are armed with good techniques. A lot of web sites are poorly designed for search engines. You can go far with just the SEO basics covered in this chapter. Be creative. Perform careful keyword research. You'll find words that others have neglected. You'll find gems that will each payoff in a small way but add up to consistent traffic in the end. One day you'll check your stats and realize that Google is shuffling new listeners your way left and right.

SUMMARY

Search engines are a great source of targeted traffic. Optimize your site to get higher search rankings for your primary keywords. Use online keyword tools to find keywords that are searched for often, but don't have too many other sites competing to get their traffic, as well.

A successful search strategy consists of on-page and off-page optimization. On-page optimization involves designing a page such that the search engines see it as having quality content that is highly relevant to a given search phrase. Off-page optimization involves getting links back to your site from relevant and authoritative pages. The more links you have back to your site, the higher it will be ranked by the search engines.

Multimedia Tutorials at PodcastingUniversity.org

For more help with the topics covered in this chapter, please visit: www.PodcastingUniversity.org/pyp/chapter4

You'll find multimedia tutorials on:

- How to research and choose the best keywords to use in your search engine campaign
- How to create web pages that will get highly ranked in the search engines
- How to gain more inbound links to your site
- How to choose a good web address for your site that will perform well in search engines
- How to track the progress of your search engine campaigns

...and more!

Attracting Listeners from Social Media Networks

CATEGORIZING CONSTANT WAVES OF CONTENT

Social media, such as podcasting, result in constant waves of new content hitting the Internet. The amount of information is staggering. How can an individual find something of interest, let alone get his own content noticed by others?

Many web users have adopted a method of categorization called tagging, an informal and collaborative way for web users to categorize information on the Internet. Millions of content creators and consumers freely choose words to describe photos, web sites, blog posts, podcasts and more. The idea is to allow the people who create and use the content to label it anyway they want.

Many social networking sites use tagging for sharing and indexing web content. *Flickr.com* allows you to post a photo of your dog and tag it "dog," "puppy," "fido," "stupid" or whatever else comes to mind. Other Flickr visitors who want to see pictures of dogs can search for all photos tagged with "dog" and they'll find yours. You can see the most popularly used Flickr tags at `flickr.com/photos/tags`.

Del.icio.us (one of the most creative web addresses around) and Furl (*furl.net*) let you bookmark sites and assign tags to them. Users can then network and share sites on similar interests. The most popular del.icio.us tags can be seen at `del.icio.us/tag`. Tagging makes it easier to find and share content on the Internet.

What does tagging mean to you as a podcaster? To fully plug into the social media revolution, you need to take advantage of tagging. There are a number of social networks that you can use to attract listeners.

TECHNORATI: WHAT'S THE BUZZ IN THE BLOGOSPHERE? AND HOW DO YOU MAKE SOME BUZZ OF YOUR OWN?

SIDENOTE: The Technorati tips covered in this chapter require that you use a blog to publish your podcast or have a podcast feed on your site's homepage. If you're not using this kind of setup to post your show, you won't be able to take advantage of the Technorati strategies outlined below.

Technorati.com is a blog and tag search engine. According to its site, it brings you "what's happening on the web right now." It indexes several social networking and media sites, as well as millions of blogs, to see what people are saying about any given subject. This information is subsequently searchable on Technorati's site.

Technorati allows keyword searching (under the *Search* tab) or searching by tag (under the *Tags* tab). Keyword searches are based on the actual text that Technorati finds in blog posts. Tag searches are based on tags provided by blog authors. Search results list individual posts according to their timeliness and degree of "authority." A blog's authority is determined by how many other blogs link to it.

If your podcast is published on a blog, as most are, your posts can be included in Technorati's search listings. This can be a great source of traffic and a way to attract new listeners interested in your topic.

CREATING A TECHNORATI ACCOUNT AND CLAIMING YOUR BLOG

The first step is to create an account. Technorati will list your blog posts in its search results whether or not you start an account with it, but there are many advantages to having an account, which we'll cover in this section. If you prefer not to start an account, you can simply ping Technorati every time you post new material and it will crawl and index your site.

Here's how to create a Technorati account:

1. Go to *www.technorati.com.*
2. Click on the *Sign Up* link.
3. Fill out the information. Click *Sign Up Now.* You'll be taken to your account page.

The next step is to claim your blog. On the account page, under the heading *Your blogs,* enter the web address for your blog and click the button. The next page will give you instructions to finish the claim.

If you use a popular blogging platform such as Wordpress, you may be able to just enter the username and password that you use to log in to and edit your blog. Then Technorati will recognize you as the owner of the blog. Technorati calls this a "quick claim."

If you're not able to do a quick claim, the process gets a little more technical. Technorati will give you a small block of code to paste into your blog's home page. The easiest way to do this is to simply copy the code into a new blog post. This may work depending on your blog software. If this works, you can delete the post once your blog is claimed.

If this doesn't work, you'll have to insert the code into your blog's design template. Check the instructions for your blogging service or software for information on how to edit your design template. You'll need to insert the code into the header or sidebar. Once the code has been added to your blog template, you can finish the claim process and Technorati will recognize you as the owner of the blog. After the claim is complete, you can delete the Technorati code snippet from your template.

When you finish the claim process, you'll be taken to a page to edit your blog's information. This also can be reached from your account page by first clicking the *View & Edit All Blog Info* link, and then on the *Configure Blog* button next to the title of the blog that you want to configure.

On the blog configuration page, Technorati asks for a description. You should enter the same description that you use in your feed, applying the tips and guidelines from the chapter on podcast directories. If Technorati tells you that the description is too long, you'll have to narrow it down, keeping as many of your keywords as you can.

On the same page you can also enter up to 20 tags to describe your podcast. Technorati may have already pulled some tags from your feed and entered them for you. These tags are used to categorize your blog and help people find you. Be sure to check the box marked *Include this blog in Technorati's Blog Finder*. This will list your blog for these tags in the Blog Finder, which people browse by subject to find weblogs that frequently post under a given tag.

You don't have to use all 20 tags. You can always change them later. Tags also can be more than one word. Read the section later, titled *How to Choose the Best Tags,* for tips on choosing your tags.

Back on your account page, it's also a good idea to upload a photo. This photo doesn't necessarily have to be a headshot of yourself; it can be a logo such as the one you use in your feed and directory listings. To upload an image file, click on *Upload a photo* and follow the instructions.

This should be a square image that is at least 64 x 64 pixels big. Keep in mind that the image will be shrunk to 64 x 64 and 20 x 20 pixel sizes. Be sure the image you choose still looks good at these sizes. If you use a portrait photo it should be a close up of your face. If you upload an image that's not square, it can end up looking distorted when Technorati resizes and stretches it. No one looks good with a mouth that's a foot wide.

By uploading an image for your blog, you're eligible to be featured on Technorati's front page. This provides a nice bump in traffic if you're one of the lucky chosen. More importantly, your logo will be displayed next to your posts in Technorati's search results. This helps your blog stand out and will increase the number of people that click through to your site.

Also, on your account page, you can edit your profile and enter a short bio. Keep in mind that you can claim multiple podcasts and blogs under one Technorati account.

SPIDER FOOD REVISITED: HOW TECHNORATI CRAWLS YOUR SITE

Remember the search engine spiders mentioned in the last chapter? Technorati also has web crawlers that browse the blog text displayed on your site. As with many other search engines, Technorati does not index the audio of your podcast. It strictly looks at the text posted to your blog. More specifically, it seems to only look at blog posts displayed on your home page.

Your show notes and other blog posts provide the fodder used to index and list your site in Technorati's search results. It's important to post show notes for each episode outlining your content with strong keywords, as discussed in the last chapter. Posting other relevant text articles between podcast episodes provides more opportunities to be listed in Technorati.

It's important to post show notes for each episode outlining your content with strong keywords.

Whenever you update you blog, you need to ping Technorati. You can do this by including Technorati in your blog's automatic ping notification list. I explained how to do this in the chapter on blog directories. The ping address for Technorati is `http://rpc.technorati.com/rpc/ping`.

If your blog software doesn't include an automatic ping feature, you can send a manual ping at `www.technorati.com/ping.html` or by using `www.pingomatic.com`. This let's Technorati know that there's new material on your blog homepage. Then Technorati will send the spiders your way to record the new content into their database.

After sending a ping, it can take a little while to get indexed, depending on how many requests Technorati has received. My experience is that you can be listed within minutes. If you consistently have problems getting indexed, you should contact Technorati for assistance.

A TWO-SIDED PLAN OF ATTACK

There are two places your podcast can be listed on Technorati's site—in the keyword search results (under the *Search* tab) and in the tag search results (under the *Tags* tab). Two different sets of criteria determine if you'll be listed in each place.

For keyword searches, you'll be listed for phrases that are found in the text of your blog post and title. If you want to be listed for the search phrase *paper airplanes,* then *paper airplanes* needs to appear in your show notes or episode title.

There may be other factors that Technorati weighs when choosing what posts to list for keyword searches, but including the phrase in your post is certainly the most obvious and easiest way to get into these listings. Also keep in mind that you can be listed for more than one phrase. You'll be listed for any keywords that Technorati finds in your blog posts.

To be listed in the tag search results, you need to include tags in your posts. I'll explain how to do this in the next section.

TAG, YOU'RE IT

There are two different ways to tag your blog posts. The first way is with post categories. Most major blog software allows you to choose one or more categories for each of your blog entries. Technorati sees these categories and uses them as tags. For example, I use Wordpress to publish my podcasts. Each of my blogs has a category called "podcast." Whenever I post a new episode, I use this category. Technorati then lists my post for "podcast" tag searches.

Some bloggers like to use lots of categories. You can use more than one for each post. If your blog software doesn't use categories or you prefer not to have a category for every tag you want to use, there's another way to tag your posts. You accomplish this by including a specific type of link in your blog entry.

Take a look at the example of tag links in a blog post on my podcast, *GothamCast.* I've tagged this episode with *new york city, nyc, manhattan, podcast, audioblog.*

Interview and show were recorded at The Living Room (Lower East Side, Manhattan).

Click Here to Listen to this Episode Now: MP3

Tags: new york city, nyc, manhattan, podcast, audioblog

These are a special kind of link that Technorati and other similar sites look for, and recognize, as tags. I place the tag links at the bottom of my blog posts with the label "Tags:" in front of them. You don't have to include this; I do it to let people know what they are.

Here's the format for a tag link in HTML code:

```
<a href="http://technorati.com/tag/tagname" rel="tag">
tagname</a>
```

Replace *tagname* with the tag phrase that you want to use. Notice there are two places to put the tag name, in the link address and in the link text. Web crawlers know the link is a tag when they see the rel="tag" in your HTML code behind the scenes. Tags on Technorati are not case sensitive. It doesn't matter if you use capital or lower case letters. The result is the same.

A tag I use often with Internet Business Mastery is entrepreneur. Here's an example of how this tag code would look:

```
<a href="http://technorati.com/tag/entrepreneur" rel="tag">
entrepreneur</a>
```

Most blog software will let you enter HTML code right into your post editor just as it appears above. To include tags in your post, simply enter the link code as it is shown above in your blog editor. Do this for each of your desired tags, replacing tagname with your phrase. I usually place the links at the bottom of my post after the show notes. Save and publish the post to your blog. The tags should show up as clickable links in your blog post.

For tags that are more than one word long, your link code should look like this:

```
<a href="http://technorati.com/tag/tagword1+tagword2"
rel="tag">tagword1 tagword2</a>
```

Notice the plus sign between each tag word in the link address. Also, notice there's no plus sign between the words later in the link text. You can have a tag with three or four words if you'd like. Just place a plus sign between each tag word in the link address.

Here's an example of the code for a multiword tag link:

```
<a href="http://technorati.com/tag/new+york+city"
rel="tag">New York City</a>
```

You might think that writing all those tag links into every blog post is about as much fun as filing your taxes. There are a couple things you can do to speed things up. I find that I use the same tags over and over. When I create a new blog entry, I usually open an old post and copy the tag links, then paste them into a new post.

There also are plugins, for certain blog software such as Wordpress, as well as bookmarklets, for browsers such as Firefox, that can help generate tags for you. An online search for *technorati tag bookmarklet* or *technorati tag plugin* will turn up more interesting information on this for you.

OTHER TAG LINK STRATEGIES

When someone clicks a tag link, they're taken to the tag search results for that phrase on the Technorati web site. You also can link to other sites, as long as the link follows the same format. Here are some examples of tags that link to sites other than Technorati:

```
<a href="http://en.wikipedia.org/wiki/gotham" rel="tag">
Gotham</a>

<a href="http://flickr.com/photos/tags/dogs"
rel="tag">Dogs</a>

<a href="http://del.icio.us/tag/help" rel="tag">Help</a>
```

This first tag links to an article on *www.wikipedia.org*. The second tag links to photos tagged with "dogs" on *www.flickr.com*. The last tag links to web site bookmarks tagged with "help" on *del.icio.us*.

Also, you don't have to put your links at the bottom of the post. This is just one of the most common ways to do it. You can put tags wherever you want. They don't even have to be grouped together. You can use them on individual links in the context of your post. For example, let's say you use the phrase "7 golf tips" in your show notes. You can make "golf tips" a tag link using the same format discussed earlier, and it will be seen by the Technorati spiders.

If you're worried about having all those links in your blog posts begging people to click away from your site, there are some tricks to help prevent that. That is another reason I place them at the bottom of the post and don't use them in the text of my show notes. Also, in your HTML code, or using Cascading Style Sheets, you can make the tag links a lighter color that is not as obvious on your background, such as light gray on white.

I do this on my sites both to downplay the links and to make things look nicer. You can take a look at how I do this on any my podcast sites:

- www.PodcastingUnderground.com
- www.InternetBusinessMastery.com
- www.GothamCast.com

I offer this tip as a suggestion, but won't go into how to do it here. You can ask a web programmer to help you, or do a little research on using different fonts in HTML or style sheets, to change the link color.

A caveat accompanies this tip. If you make the links too light, or even the same color as the background (to the point where they're not easily visible), Google and other search engines might think you're up to some funny business and penalize your site's ranking. Avoid going too far with it.

To maximize your traffic from Technorati, it's important to pick the right tags.

HOW TO CHOOSE THE BEST TAGS: TEN TIPS FOR TERRIFIC TECHNORATI TRAFFIC

To maximize your traffic from Technorati, it's important to pick the right tags. Here's my list of tips for choosing the best tags:

> 1. **Choose Relevant Tags**
> No one likes the "bait and switch." Don't throw in an irrelevant tag just because you think it will get a lot of searches. This will just make people mad and it won't create any fans, let alone listeners.

You don't want just any traffic. You want people who will convert to listeners. Choose relevant tags that will draw visitors interested in your kind of content. Run a search in Technorati for a tag and see if your podcast would fit in with the results. Also, make sure the results for that tag are focused, as indicated in the next tip.

2. **Mostly Use Tags That Have Two or More Words**
As with targeting keyword ranking in search engines, it's easier to get noticed for a tag that contains more than one word. In addition, people who search for longer tag phrases tend to know what they want and make more targeted visitors. They're more likely to convert to a listener.

For example, I can use the internet tag for *Internet Business Mastery,* but this is not a focused phrase. The results contain a wide range of topics. I'm much more likely to get listeners by using tags such as *internet business, internet marketing* or *internet based business.*

3. **Don't Break New Ground**
You can make up and use any tag. You could tag your podcast with "llama herding," if you wanted. It doesn't do any good, though, if no one is using, or searching for, that phrase. Stick to tags that are already being used. The idea with tagging is that social networks will settle into using certain tags more than others to describe a given category. Stick to what has become the norm. Perform a tag search for your phrase in Technorati to be sure it is already getting used.

4. **Use Synonyms Where Appropriate**
There's more than one way to describe something. *Internet business* can also be described as *online business* or *web business.* Since all three of these tags are used often on Technorati, they all get used in my posts on *Internet Business Mastery.* Make sure you use synonyms, where appropriate.

5. **Use Technorati's Related Tags**
When you perform a tag search in Technorati, you'll see a list of other related tags listed above the results. This is a good way to jog your imagination and get ideas for other tags to use.

6. **Look at Technorati's Most Popular Tags**
Technorati lists the tags that are currently getting the most searches on its home page as well as at www.technorati.com/tags. Look through these tags for any topics around which you could plan an episode, and then use the tag in your show notes.

7. **Anticipate and Follow Events and Media Stories**
If an imminent event or news story is likely to get public attention, predicate a podcast on it. I offered frequent updates from the 2005 Portable Media Expo on The Podcasting Underground. I used tags such as *portable media expo, pme* and *podcast expo* for these episodes and blog posts. These measures helped attract a considerable number of new visitors and subscribers to my site.

8. **Use Tags That Are Ranked in Google**
Do a search for the tag phrase in Google. If the Technorati page for that tag appears on the first couple pages of results, that's a good sign. Technorati will draw traffic from Google for that tag and you can draw traffic from Technorati.

Take "podcast expo," as an example. If you search for this phrase in Google, on the first page of results is a link to Technorati's page for this tag:

technorati.com/tags/podcast+expo

An easy way to check if Technorati tags are listed in Google's top rankings is with the ranking tool at www.nichebot.com/ranking/. Not only can you use this tool to check the rank for your own site, you can check other sites as well.

To use this tool, enter the list of tag phrases that you want to check. Then enter www.technorati.com as the domain. Run the search. If you see Technorati appear in the top 20 for any given phrase, it's a good idea to use the tag.

9. **Choose Tags Used by Popular Podcasts and Blogs in Your Niche**
By finding, and using, the same tags as popular podcasts and blogs in your niche, you're joining an Internet conversation. You should link from your own posts to specific entries in these blogs. This is bound to invite links back to you, bringing traffic your way.

10. Use Abbreviations Where Appropriate
Sometimes abbreviations get adopted as tags. An example of this is "pme" for portable media expo or "nyc" for New York City. If this is the case, you should follow suit, and use the abbreviations as well as the full phrases.

HOW MANY IS TOO MANY?

When do you have too many tags in a post? There's no set answer to this question. Some bloggers and podcasters take the stance that you should add as many tags as you want, as long as they're relevant. This may be fine, but let me share a few cautionary insights from my own experience.

First, too many tags can make a mess of your blog post. Also, there's no solid proof, but it is speculated that Technorati could consider you a tag spammer if you use too many. In this case, you could be barred completely from being listed in its search results. Even if it's not doing this now, it could in the future. Technorati takes whatever precautions necessary to preserve the validity of its searches.

Stick to 10 or fewer tags for each post, if you want to play it safe. This quantity is sufficient for your tags to serve their purpose. You don't need to go overboard with tagging. If you find yourself tagging your cat and your grandma, you've definitely gone too far.

LAZY WEB CRAWLERS

Because Technorati seems to only crawl your home page each time it receives a ping, any posts that you want to be indexed must appear on that page. The Technorati spiders don't follow links to other pages on your blog. It's probably a union thing. Actually, Technorati probably does this to optimize the efficiency of its indexing resources.

However, once a post is indexed, it will stay in the Technorati database even after it slips off the front page of your blog. Your blog is probably set up to only display a certain number of your most recent entries on the home page. You can usually change this number in the blog options of your blogging software. Check the instructions for your blogging service for more information on how to do this.

Here's a nice little trick to get some of your podcast and blog archives listed. Go into your blog configuration and change it to display as many listings on the front page as you dare. (That said, don't include so many that your home page takes a millennium to load.) Then ping Technorati. You may need to wait a few hours to a day, or more. Eventually, those ravenous spiders will come and devour the feast you have provided.

This way you'll get more of your blog indexed. However, Technorati may list all these posts as brand new, since they were just crawled. They'll all have the same timestamp on them in the Technorati listings. That's not a big deal, though. The point is that all that info is now in their database. In addition, Technorati will give you credit for links to your old blog posts. This will increase your blog's authority and ranking on its site. Once your blog archives are indexed, you can change the number of posts on the home page back to what it was before.

The lazy web crawler hitch also brings another potential pitfall. Your blog software may have a feature where it only displays an excerpt of a blog post, and then a "more" link that takes the reader to the rest of the post. Depending on where you place your tags, this could cause problems.

If the tags are at the bottom of the post, but the bottom of the post doesn't appear on the home page, the web crawlers probably won't see them. Depending on your blog software, they may not be in the feed either.

If your blog is currently using this "more" feature, sometimes also called a bump, turn it off in your blog software options. Either that, or change the placement of your tags to the top of the post. For many reasons, this is not an ideal place to put them, but it will work if you insist on using bumps in your posts.

WHAT IF YOU'RE STILL NOT SHOWING UP ON TECHNORATI?

Now that you're using tags and pinging Technorati, you should start showing up in the search listings for the tags and keywords you're using in your posts. It can take several minutes to a few hours for your posts to start showing up after pinging Technorati. It all depends on how long it takes the spiders to come calling.

You should check the Technorati listings on occasion to be sure you're still appearing in search results. Go to the site and do a few keyword and tag searches for your phrases. Blogs have been known to disappear from Technorati searches. If you're getting traffic from them, you don't want the well to suddenly run dry.

If you're still not showing up in the Technorati results, and you have carefully followed all the tips discussed above to make sure your tags appear on the home page, there are a couple more things you can try to remedy this disappearing act. First, validate your feed at `www.feedvalidator.org` and fix any errors. Errors in your feed create hurdles for web crawlers.

Also, you can email Technorati support and let them know about the problem. They may have an explanation. Technorati has been known to mistakenly flag legitimate blogs as spam content. In this case, support will have to fix it for you.

I've also seen unexpected problems arise from redirecting a home page to another web address, which sometimes confuses spiders and prevents them from following through to see the content. Maybe Technorati doesn't pay or train its staff enough. But in all likelihood, the problem stems from an oversight in the way Technorati has programmed its crawlers. Hopefully, Technorati will update its spider software to finally solve this shortcoming.

If you still are not showing up or getting a response from Technorati, you can delete the claim to your blog and do it over again. I would only try this as a last resort. Sometimes this will fix things.

TIPS FOR STANDING OUT IN THE TECHNORATI SEARCH RESULTS

Let's take a look at the makeup of Technorati's search listings to see how you can stand out and increase your chances of getting new listeners to click through to your site.

The first thing you see in a Technorati search result is the title of the blog post. Below the

> **Consulting for Shure Microphones Part 2**
> 🔍 💬 ➕ By Jason Van Orden in 27 days ago
> Consulting for Shure Microphones Part 2 Saturday, March 25th, 2006 My interview with Shure Microphones on **podcasting** is now available online ... The **Podcasting Underground**, Internet Business Mastery and the critically acclaimed GothamCast. All your ... . They also posted the musician version of the **Podcasting** 101 article based on my consultation
>
> **Podcasting Underground on Front Page of iTunes**
> 🔍 💬 ➕ By Jason Van Orden in Podcasting Underground: Podcas... 29 days ago
> **Podcasting Underground** on Front Page of iTunes March 23rd, 2006 3:57 am (Miscellaneous) I just noticed that **Podcasting Underground** is featured on the front page of iTunes' podcast directory with other great podcasts on **podcasting**. I'm going to stop now before this post gets any

post title is the blog's name. This is another place where a catchy episode title and podcast name will pull in more potential listeners. If the title of your episode is something like *7 Ways to Prevent Identity Theft,* someone searching Technorati for "identity theft" is likely to click it. When someone clicks the title, they're taken to your site.

Technorati also tracks how many links a blog has to it from other weblogs, indicated by a green icon resembling a comic strip speech balloon. If you place your mouse over this icon, a number will appear. This helps searchers find the most popular and relevant information.

If you click the icon, you'll get a list of other sources that link to that blog. This is how Technorati determines your blog's level of "authority." The search results can be listed in order of authority, in addition to chronologically.

It's a good idea to encourage, and ask for, links to your podcast's blog. Many of your listeners may have blogs or web sites. The best favor an avid fan can do for you is to mention your podcast on their site or blog with a link. This generates traffic to your podcast and boosts your "authority" in the eyes of search engines, such as Technorati. Another great way to get links is to create regular quality content to which people want to link.

Looking back at the search listing, you can see it also specifies how long ago the post was made. This can be measured in minutes or days, depending on how often the topic is blogged about. The most recent blog posts are listed at the top. The newer your post, the closer it will appear to the top.

The last piece in the listing is an excerpt of the post. This is simply the first few sentences of your blog post or show notes. If your title piques someone's interest, they'll read this excerpt. The excerpt should entice the searcher to click through to your site.

Pay close attention to what you include in the first few lines of your show notes. Phrases like *Episode #10, Click Here to Download This Episode* or *Hosted by Vern* won't generate interest in your podcast episode. You need to provide concise and punchy info in these first few lines of your blog post that will make someone want to hear more.

You'll also see some search results with a small image next to it. This is shown if the blogger has created a Technorati account and added a photo to their profile. I mentioned earlier that a photo or logo helps you stand out, because it draws the eye.

SOCIAL ESPIONAGE

Do you want to know what your podcast peers are doing to generate buzz? You can search Technorati for the name of a podcast or a podcast's web address to see who is talking about, or linking to, them. If someone is getting frequent links, take a look at what they are doing to get ideas for building your own traffic. This is a good way to find link partners and key players in your niche. It also helps you keep an eye on your competitor's buzz.

DEL.ICIO.US SOCIAL BOOKMARKING

Del.icio.us (del.icio.us) is a very useful site for storing bookmarks to web pages that interest you. Del.icio.us also lets you tag your bookmarks for sharing and finding new sites. It's another great social networking site for getting your link in front of people with similar interests. Yahoo bought del.icio.us in 2005, which underscores the growth of social tagging and bookmarking.

The front page of del.icio.us has a list of recently bookmarked web addresses, as well as the most popular tags and sites associated with those tags.

To get a list of the most recent web addresses with a particular tag, enter it into the search box. Another way to do this is to enter a web address with the format del.icio.us/tag/tagname replacing tagname with the category that interests you. For example, del.icio.us/tag/cooking would take you to a list of popular sites tagged with the word cooking.

You can start your own list of saved bookmarks by first creating an account. This is done by clicking on the register link on the home page of del.icio.us. The username you choose will determine the web address which points to your collection of bookmarks. Your bookmark will be del.icio.us/username.

del.icio.us / search
your bookmarks | inbox | links for you | post

Search results for **cooking**

Your items

showing 1 - 3 of 12525

» More results in your items

Everyone's items

showing 1 - 10 of 12525

« previous | next »

Cooking For Engineers save this
to cooking food recipes blog geek ... saved by 2996 other people

All Recipes – complete resource for recipes, cooking tips and food save this
to recipes cooking food reference recipe ... saved by 1345 other people

For example, you can see a list of bookmarks I've saved at del.icio.us/jasonvo. If you want to see a list of my podcasting related links, you can go to del.icio.us/jasonvo/podcasting. I also post and tag links that I think will interest my *GothamCast* listeners at `del.icio.us/gothamcast`.

Once you've created an account, you can start saving links by logging in and clicking on the post link. Enter the web address that you'd like to save to your account and click the save button. On the next page you'll be asked for a description, notes and tags for the link. The description is like a title for the bookmark and is displayed as the text for your link. Enter the site name or a brief description for the link. The notes field is for entering thoughts about the link. Then enter the tags that you want to associate with the bookmark. The information for a bookmark can be changed or deleted later.

Enter as many tags as you'd like, separating each word with a space. If you enter a multi-word tag, each word will be used as a separate single-word tag. Del.icio.us doesn't use multiword tags as you would see in Technorati. To tag a link with something like new york city, I combine the words and enter newyorkcity.

Use the tips I listed above in the *How to Choose the Best Tags* section for selecting del.icio.us tags as well.

TASTY TRAFFIC FROM DEL.ICIO.US BOOKMARKS

Getting your site, blog posts and podcast episodes saved and tagged in del.icio.us generates traffic to your show. Here are five ways to make this happen:

1. If your site or one of your episodes is bookmarked by enough people, it will show up in the most popular listings for corresponding tags.

2. Links to del.icio.us tag pages are sometimes ranked well in search engines such as Google. If you appear on these listing pages, you'll siphon some of this traffic to your site.

3. Just about every page on del.icio.us has an RSS feed.
    Some people subscribe to the feed for the most recent
    and/or most popular tags on topics that interest them.

4. Some web sites syndicate the feed for the most recent
    or popular bookmarks from a given del.icio.us tag
    page. This gets your link on other sites and in front of
    potential listeners.

5. If you include useful links on your topic, people will
    subscribe to your feed to get your latest bookmarks,
    including the ones to your own site.

Save your home page's web address to your del.icio.us account. Also,
each time you post a new episode, save the link to the blog post to
del.icio.us. Your links will start appearing in listings and searches on
del.icio.us.

Another little-used strategy that has generated traffic for me is to post
and tag the direct link to the audio file for each episode (e.g., `www.your-podcast.com/mp3s/yourpodcastfile.mp3`). Tag the episode with relevant
words as well as with mp3, podcast, podcasts and podcasting. Some
del.icio.us users like to subscribe to the feed for these tags (e.g.,
`del.icio.us/rss/tag/mp3`) in their podcatcher to find new
content to listen to.

ENCOURAGE OTHERS TO BOOKMARK YOUR EPISODES AND MAKE IT EASY FOR THEM TO DO SO

Feel free to ask your audience to
bookmark your episodes in
del.icio.us. Make it easy for your
listeners to save and tag your site
or blog posts. I suggest including
an *Add to del.icio.us* link at the
bottom of each post. When
someone clicks this link, they'll be
taken to del.icio.us to save the
bookmark to their account.

del.icio.us / jasonvo /

your bookmarks | inbox | links for you | post

url http://www.podcastingunderground.com/

description podcasting tips for podcasters

notes

tags howtopodcast podcast podcasting

save

Here's HTML code for adding this kind of link to your blog post or web site:

```
<a
href="http://del.icio.us/post?url=webaddress&title=descriptio
n&tags=tag1 tag2 tag3">Add to del.icio.us</a>
```

After `url=`, replace webaddress with the address for that blog post (e.g., `http://www.yoursite.com/blogpost.html`). This is the web address being saved and tagged in del.icio.us. In place of description, enter a suggested title for the bookmark. This should either be the title of that episode or simply something like *Podcast Name Episode #X*.

Finally, after `tags=`, where you see tag1 tag2 tag3, enter tags that you would like them to use when they save the bookmark. This can be one tag or as many as you'd like, with a space in between each word. By suggesting tags like this, you increase your chances of gaining popularity for given tags.

Depending on what blog software you use, you can probably enter this HTML code right into your blog post editor. If your Technorati tag links are at the bottom of the post, include the del.icio.us link just above that. Having a link like this after each post makes it easy for a site visitor to bookmark a post in del.icio.us and increases your chances of being seen on their site.

If you use FeedBurner, it offers a feature for placing an *Add to del.icio.us* link to your feed at the bottom of each post. Someone will see this if they view your feed in a newsreader. Since most people will probably just use your feed in their podcatcher and not a newsreader, they may not see the link. However, it doesn't hurt to turn the feature on. Here's how:

1. Log in to your FeedBurner account and click on the name of the podcast to which you want to add this feature.
2. Click on the *Optimize* tab.
3. Click on the *Feedflare* button.

4. Under the *Feed* column, check the box next to *Add to del.icio.us*. At the bottom of the page you can see a preview of what the link will look like in your feed.

5. If *Feedflare* is not yet activated, click the activate button.

6. Click the *Save* button.

MORE BOOKMARKING

If you just can't get enough of all this online socialization, *Furl.net* is another site that is great for bookmarking your posts and audio files to get links in front of potential listeners. Furl has several differences from del.icio.us—not to mention a name that is easier to type. Furl attracts a different crowd.

Some people prefer Furl because it saves a copy of the page that you bookmark, making it a little more like a filing cabinet. They call it your "personal web." Furl also includes privacy features that del.icio.us does not. Instead of tags, Furl has categories and keywords. When saving your bookmarks, use the categories as you would tags.

TIPS FOR QUICK POSTING TO DEL.ICIO.US AND FURL

Here are a few ideas for making it quick and easy to save bookmarks to del.icio.us and Furl:

1. If you use the Firefox Internet browser, you can download a del.icio.us extension that adds buttons to your toolbar. This allows you to tag sites and access your account at the click of a button. The extension can be downloaded from `del.icio.us/help/firefox/extension`.

2. There are a number of bookmarklets for Firefox that allow quick tagging of web pages in del.icio.us and Furl. A search in Google for *delicious bookmarklet* will turn up some options. You can get Furl bookmarklets at `http://www.furl.net/tools.jsp`.

3. Furl has a toolbar that can be added to your browser. It's available at `http://www.furl.net/tools.jsp`.

4. If you use Wordpress, there's a plugin for bookmarking in del.icio.us, as well as Furl, called Sociable. It can be found at `http://push.cx/sociable`.

SUMMARY

Tagging is a method of categorization that has been adopted by web users as an informal and collaborative way to categorize information and content on the Internet. You can use tagging and popular social networks such as del.icio.us and Technorati to promote your podcast.

Create a Technorati account and submit your feed for indexing. Include tag links in your show notes and ping Technorati each time you post an episode to your blog. Your podcast will then be included in Technorati's tag search engine.

Del.icio.us is a social bookmarking site. Use del.icio.us to bookmark each post and audio file for an episode of your podcast. Encourage your listeners to do the same. *Furl.net* is another social bookmarking site that you can use.

Multimedia Tutorials at PodcastingUniversity.org

For more help with the topics covered in this chapter, please visit: `www.PodcastingUniversity.org/pyp/chapter5`

You'll find multimedia tutorials on:

- Creating a Technorati account
- Tagging your show notes and blog posts
- Finding the best tags to use in your posts
- Conducting social espionage to see what others are saying about your show
- Tagging your podcasts in del.icio.us

...and more!

Strategies for Getting Exposure in Other Podcasts

TYPES OF CROSS-PROMOTION AUDIO

Podcasters always need more audio content for their podcast. They love using audio from other sources that adds value to their show. This audio can entail comments, testimonials, guest hosts and interviews, to name a few. It stirs things up so the podcaster isn't doing all the talking. It also adds diverse voices and enhances the "community" aspect of the podcast.

Think about it. If someone sent you an interesting thought, insightful question or raving review, you'd want to play it on your show. Submitting these kinds of audio clips to other podcasts is a great way to help promote your own show. It's a generally accepted practice, and even encouraged, to include your podcast's name and web address in any audio you submit for play. But as with any of the ideas in this book, you have to go about it the right way.

If you take the time to prepare good clips and send them to the right people, very often they'll get played. By submitting to podcasts that are in the same genre as your own, your message is sure to reach people who are prone to enjoy your show as well.

There are several kinds of audio that you can produce and submit for play on other podcasts.

There are several kinds of audio that you can produce and submit for play on other podcasts:

1. A promo for your podcast.
2. A comment that expounds on, or responds to, something that was mentioned.
3. Feedback for the podcaster—especially when they ask for it.
4. A question that adds to the "conversation."
5. A testimonial stating why you like the podcast.
6. A podcast ID for another podcast, akin to a radio station identification (e.g., "You're listening to the XYZ Podcast").

You can also offer to do an interview or co-host an episode. Any of these ideas allow you to expose other listeners to your ideas and, at the very least, to give them your name, web address and a quick teaser to lure them in. As I explain below, there are several methods to keep in mind when preparing audio clips for other podcasters.

HOW TO SUBMIT YOUR AUDIO

The easiest way to submit a comment or other audio is through the podcaster's voicemail line. Many podcasts maintain a phone line specifically for listeners to call and leave comments or feedback.

That said, many podcasters have a "love-hate" relationship with voicemail. It's the easiest way for listeners to speak up. Most people don't know how to record themselves, but they know how to pick up the phone and leave a message. However, the audio quality is less than ideal. Podcasters tend to endure the questionable audio to make the process easy for their audience, and then clean up the phone noise and volume as best they can.

On the other hand, you should have all the equipment and know-how to produce a top-notch clip. Record the comment yourself, then give it to the podcaster as a high-quality audio file. This will greatly increase the chance that it gets played. Make sure it's ready for podcasters to easily drop into their show. If they have to fuss with it at all, they may not bother with it.

THE NIFTY NINE

Follow my nine tips for producing and sending audio clips:

1. **Normalize the Audio**
   To "normalize" means to bring up the volume to a set level. Most audio recording and processing programs have a normalization feature. There should be an option to increase the volume until the loudest point in the clip has the highest volume possible.

   If you don't have a normalization feature, you can simply turn up the audio in the file as much as you can without causing it to clip (cut off the tops of the waveforms by going higher than the allowed maximum level).

   If your audio is weak and has a low level, podcasters will either have to fix it or just won't play it. They want to keep the volume consistent throughout their show. If your comment comes in and the listener has to strain to hear you, you're not doing anyone any favors.

2. **Don't Send Huge Files By Email**
   A lot of email accounts won't allow you to send or receive files that are too large. Depending on the length of your audio clip, the file could be several megabytes big. You probably need to convert it to MP3 format to reduce the file size. Regardless, I don't recommend sending the file by email. You'll just be filling up the recipient's email storage space.

   If possible, upload the file to your web hosting and then send the podcaster a link from where the clip can be downloaded. Another alternative is to use a service, such as *YouSendIt.com.* YouSendIt allows you to upload a large file through their web site and sends a download link to your recipient.

3. **Send Audio Files of the Highest Quality Possible**
The podcaster will insert your audio clip into the master audio file for his episode. This is a problem if you send an MP3 that has already been compressed quite a bit (reduced in size). The audio quality of your clip will have already been reduced by your MP3 conversion. When the podcaster converts his podcast to MP3, your audio will get compressed again and could produce audio that doesn't sound very good.

    Send as high a quality audio file as possible. The best quality audio is a .wav file that contains all the original data. However, .wav files are usually quite large. If you're fairly sure that the podcaster has a fast connection and will have no problem with a large file, go ahead and send the .wav file. Otherwise, you should convert it to MP3 format.

    You probably convert your own podcast audio to MP3 format encoded at 64 to 128 kbps. This is the bit rate (kilobits per second). The higher the bit rate, the better the quality, but the bigger the file. When you record an audio clip to send to another podcaster, I suggest encoding at a bit rate of at least 192 kbps. This allows other podcasters to insert the clip and compress their own podcasts, without your clip sounding like nails on a chalkboard.

4. **Plug Your Show**
That's the whole point of creating and submitting the audio clip. Whether it's a comment, question, feedback or otherwise, be sure to mention the name of your podcast and your web address. A way to do this is to start out your comment by saying, "This is Bob from the Yodeling Showdown Podcast online at YodelMaster.com. I just wanted to say that..." You can even slip in a quick description of your podcast to entice people more.

5. **Keep it Short**
Keep the length of your audio clip between 30 seconds and two minutes, tops. Don't take more time than you need to make your point. The podcaster has to keep in mind his audience's attention span. If your clip will put them to sleep, he won't play it.

6. **Keep it Interesting**
   Ask yourself, "If it was for my podcast, would I want to play this clip?" No one wants to bore listeners. Offer useful insights. Be witty, interesting or both.

7. **Have No Shame**
   A little shameless kissing up can work wonders. No matter what kind of audio clip it is, briefly tell the other podcaster how great they are. Any podcaster loves this. Playing your comment on the show will be an ego boost for him. He'll have a hard time resisting.

8. **Send A Personalized Email to the Podcaster**
   Accompany or preface your audio clip with an email explaining who you are and what is included in the audio clip. Make it clear that you know something about the podcaster and the show. You don't want it to appear like nothing more than a self-serving move. Point out why the audio contributes something of value to their show.

9. **Sweeten the Deal**
   One way to increase the chances of getting your audio played is to offer to play their promo or interview them on your podcast, in exchange. The great thing about interviewing another podcaster is that they'll probably tell their audience about it, which will bring more listeners to your podcast.

PODCAST IDS

A very simple way to get played is to record a brief podcast ID for someone else's podcast. Podcasters like to start their show with an audio clip from a listener or other podcaster that announces their podcast. Here is an example of a typical podcast ID:

"This is *YourName* from *YourPodcast* at *PodcastAddress.com,* where we discuss *DescriptionOfPodcast.* You're listening to the *NameOfOtherPodcast.* Now, here's your host *NameOfOtherPodcaster.*"

That's a plain vanilla example, but you get the idea. You certainly can be more creative. In fact, it's best if you are.

PODCAST PROMOS

Podcasters tend to be a very collaborative and helpful bunch. Many like to play promos for podcasts that will interest their listeners. For the most part, there seems to be little feeling of competition.

This is where you can really let your creativity shine. Come up with an entertaining and interesting clip to promote your podcast. Put a little production time into it, rather than just rattling off a stale script. Also, remember to give people a reason to check out your show. After hearing your promo, they should know why they want to give up some of their valuable time to check out your podcast.

A good way to find podcasts to which you can send your audio clips is to simply browse the same podcast directory categories that list your podcast. I look for podcasts that seem to be a good match, then subscribe to the feed and listen to a couple of shows. If I think our audiences would be compatible, I email the host and propose a promo exchange.

You also can post your promo on Podcast Pickle (`podcastpickle.com`) in your profile, and find other promos there to play in your own show. Kiptronic (`kiptronic.com`) offers a promo exchange network to help you find other podcasts with which to exchange promos.

Here are three more sites where podcasters exchange promos:

- www.podcastpromos.com
- www.digitalpodcast.com/forum/viewforum.php?f=32
- www.podcastspots.com/Add-Podcast-Promo.aspx

Rather than give you a script of what to say or an example of one of my promos, I'm going to suggest that you visit any of the sites I mentioned above. Browse around and listen to several promos from other podcasts. This should give you plenty of ideas and get the creative juices flowing.

HOW AN AUDIO COMMENT IN A PODCAST STARTED THIS VERY BOOK YOU ARE READING

You might have heard of a podcast called Podcast Brothers (podcastbrothers.com), where Tim and Emile Bourquin discuss the business of podcasting. I listen to every episode of their show. In one episode, they talked about several ways to promote a podcast. They provided useful insights, but additional tips came to my mind that I thought they would find interesting.

I immediately hopped on the mic and recorded a two-minute audio clip that suggested more promotion ideas. I posted the MP3 to my site and sent an email to Tim with a link to the file. On their next episode, not only did they play my audio clip, they also discussed it for several minutes.

The immediate benefit was a nice influx of traffic to my site, but it got even better. One listener heard my comments, went to my site, downloaded an ebook I had published there and liked it enough that he made a point to meet me at the Podcast and Portable Media Expo. He expressed interest in having me write a book on podcast promotion for his company to publish.

Now, I'm not saying everyone will end up with book deals, but it does demonstrate one of the mantras I live by—make some noise and people will listen.

SUMMARY

A great way to promote your podcast is by contributing audio to other podcasts. Podcasters are always interested in playing audio from outside sources to mix things up and keep their show interesting. You can get exposure for your podcast by submitting a promo, comment, testimonial or podcast ID.

Make it easy for the podcaster to use your audio. Create a clip that is interesting and will add value to their podcast. Keep it short and to the point. Normalize the audio. Most of all, remember to mention your podcast. Submit the audio by uploading the audio file to your site and emailing the podcaster a link to download it from.

There are several sites where you can exchange promos with other podcasters, such as podcastpickle.com, kiptronic.com and podcastpromos.com. Browse these sites to find promo partners and to get ideas for your own promo.

Multimedia Tutorials at PodcastingUniversity.org

For more help with the topics covered in this chapter, please visit: www.PodcastingUniversity.org/pyp/chapter6

You'll find multimedia tutorials on:

- Creating audio promos
- Finding promo exchange partners

As well as further resources such as:

- A list of additional places to post your promos
- Example promos
- Example scripts for promos

...and more!

How to Get Exposure in the Press

THE POWER OF PRESS

So far, we have only discussed strategies for promoting your podcast online. Although this is a great foundation, it's only one slice of the pie. There are numerous ways to promote your podcast offline, as well. Did you know that the best advertising available in the media is free? In this chapter, we'll talk about how to get this kind of coveted promotion.

The free exposure that comes from an article or interview mentioning your podcast is even more powerful than a full-page ad in a newspaper or a 30-second spot on TV. This kind of promotion is better because it is:

1. Free
2. Seen by a lot more people
3. More credible

To get the same benefits with an ad would cost hundreds to thousands of dollars. Moreover, people read and believe news stories. They're more skeptical about ads. Press coverage is so powerful that some marketing even tries to mimic it.

Have you seen those late night infomercials that imitate the look and feel of news programs? (Come on; admit it. You've watched them. Don't worry. You're not as crazy as I am. I watch them on purpose. Yes, on purpose. I'm a marketing geek, and as such, I'm always trolling for new ideas.) Infomercials do this because it comes across as more credible. People have been trained over time to pay attention and give more credence to news-like exposure. It makes more of an impression on people's minds.

There's also an instant mystique that comes along with being mentioned in the news. If you're on the news, you must be cool, right? People think that you wouldn't be in the press if you were a jerk. Well, unless you're being frog-marched into a courthouse with a trench coat thrown over your head.

Even if the press is negative, it attracts attention. You've heard the phrase "there's no such thing as bad press." Why do you think celebrities perform all those crazy antics? They want to get their name in the media and keep it there. They hire people that do nothing but come up with strategies for getting more press.

You can get your name and your podcast in the newspapers, in magazines and on television, too. You don't have to throw a tantrum on an airplane, jump up and down on Oprah's couch or date someone 30 years younger than you, either. You just write what's new and interesting about your podcast. The media are constantly looking for stories that will interest their readers, listeners or viewers.

I learned the power of this when I was in a rock band. A rock band's life depends on making noise in the scene and generating buzz. The press is the key instrument for doing this. Using newsworthy stories, my band was the only band to get exposure and play on the local top 40 Clear Channel Communications radio station. It's nearly impossible for an independent local band to get radio play on a Clear Channel-owned radio station. The politics of the industry create high barriers to entry.

So how did we do it? We used newsworthy stories about our band. This station's morning show needed interesting material, and we gave it to them. When we went to Los Angeles to talk to record labels, we let them know about it. They brought us on air to perform live and talk about the experience. When we had a big show opening for popular bands, we let them know about it. They had us on air to play our music live and talk about our concert. We did the same thing when we made it to the finals of a local talent contest. A story was written in a local newspaper chronicling the achievement. We leveraged interesting stories to get press exposure.

> The media are always in need of stories. You get exposure by giving them what they need.

What you don't want to do is call an editor and just say, "Hey, please write about my new podcast." You have to appeal to the fact that the editors and reporters want to deliver valuable and interesting content to their readers. The media are always in need of stories. You get exposure by giving them what they need.

YOUR STORY IN INKY BLACK AND WHITE

So, what's your story? The great thing is that just being a podcaster is a great springboard. Podcasting is new and interesting. It's generating a lot of buzz right now. Have your local news outlets talked about podcasting at all? They may not know that much about it yet. You are the perfect person to educate your local newspaper or TV about podcasting. Emphasize that podcasting is a new technology. The media like to keep their readers informed about new technologies, and podcasting is still relatively new. I've been interviewed just because I was a podcaster who could talk about what was going on in podcasting.

What's interesting about your podcast or you, as a podcaster? Find a newsworthy angle about your podcast. Contact the media and let them know about it. Here are 10 questions and ideas to help you come up with a news angle that you can pitch to the media:

1. Did you just launch a new kind of podcast that hasn't been done before? Launching a unique podcast is a newsworthy story. If you have come up with a use for podcasting that hasn't been tried before, you have a good news story.

2. Are you the first podcaster in your area? If you have the first podcast in your town, the local paper would be interested to know about it.

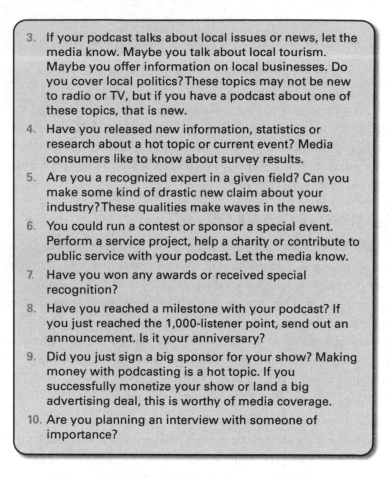

3. If your podcast talks about local issues or news, let the media know. Maybe you talk about local tourism. Maybe you offer information on local businesses. Do you cover local politics? These topics may not be new to radio or TV, but if you have a podcast about one of these topics, that is new.

4. Have you released new information, statistics or research about a hot topic or current event? Media consumers like to know about survey results.

5. Are you a recognized expert in a given field? Can you make some kind of drastic new claim about your industry? These qualities make waves in the news.

6. You could run a contest or sponsor a special event. Perform a service project, help a charity or contribute to public service with your podcast. Let the media know.

7. Have you won any awards or received special recognition?

8. Have you reached a milestone with your podcast? If you just reached the 1,000-listener point, send out an announcement. Is it your anniversary?

9. Did you just sign a big sponsor for your show? Making money with podcasting is a hot topic. If you successfully monetize your show or land a big advertising deal, this is worthy of media coverage.

10. Are you planning an interview with someone of importance?

GETTING THE ATTENTION OF THE MEDIA WITH PRESS RELEASES

How do you let the media know that you have a good story for them? You send out a press release. A press release is a concise statement about your newsworthy story. It's not a sales or ad pitch. The idea is to provide them with a story that is primarily useful to them, but also mentions your podcast. If they think the story will interest their audience, they'll use it. They might even contact you for an interview or more information.

When fellow New Yorkers Roy and Marina Kamen of *MARINA's Walking & Aerobics Podcast* (MARINASpodcast.com), won the best Health and Fitness Podcast Award in 2005, they sent out a press release to let the media know.

Health & Fitness Podcast Producer/Developer MARINA takes 1st place at World's First People's Choice Podcast Awards

NEW YORK, NY July 25, 2005 - MARINA's Walking & Aerobics Workout Podcast (www.marinaspodcast.com) takes first place in Health & Fitness Podcast category at the first People's Choice Podcast Awards (www.podcastwards.com), according to Podcast Connect (www.podcastconnect.com).

MARINA, co-owner of Kamen Entertainment Group/MRK Records, is best known for her musical compositions, vocals and countless releases over the past twenty years in the record industry, advertising and fitness communities. MARINA's fitness development clients have included QVC (Urban Rebounding), Jackie Chan's CableFlex and Strive Enterprises (Circuit Training). MARINA has been covered in The New York Times, Billboard and Family Circle Magazines, as well as being featured on The Discovery Health Network, Noggin and PBS.

MARINA is a forty-something-year-old mother of three children who lost 100 POUNDS. MARINA is designing workout podcast programs for walking, running, aerobics, bodysculpting, stretching, relaxation and motivation.

"A large percentage of the population use iPods for working out. You see people using them walking outside, and in the gym" says Roy Kamen, President of Kamen Entertainment Group. "MARINA's Workout Podcasts have widespread appeal. We've logged over 70,000 MP3 downloads of MARINA's podcasts".

MARINA writes, produces, records and sings all of the songs in her Workout Podcasts. MARINA delivers you motivational tips that represent her own personal battle of the bulge. Slip on your headphones and fire up MARINA's Workout Podcasts.

"Working out doesn't have to be a homework assignment, it should be fun!" says MARINA. "I hope my Podcasts will get people up and moving and help fight the obesity epidemic we are seeing today around the world."

MARINA has created forty-two different workout podcasts to, as MARINA says, help you "Have Better Times Workin On Out, Now!"

MARINA's Workout Podcasts are available for free on Apple iTunes 4.9 and at www.marinaspodcast.com.

Also available are "MARINA's Kool Car Radio Podcast" for children and "MARINA's Artists Studio Podcast" for aspiring actors and performing artists.

Kamen Entertainment Group/MRK Records is an award-winning entertainment company housing 11,000 sq. ft. of recording and production facilities located in Times Square NYC.

###

According to Roy Kamen, this story was picked up by over 20 online and print media sources and resulted in 500,000 downloads of their podcast.

One of my favorite podcasts is Dailysonic (dailysonic.com). Not only do they have interesting content, they are also doing very unique things with their podcast. Dailysonic devised technology that allows a listener to customize his own listening experience. He can choose what segments he wants to get, in what order and on what day. This is the power of podcasting at its best. They were the first to offer this technology on their site. As soon as they released it, they sent out a press release.

There's bound to be something newsworthy about your show. Find it or make it happen, and then tell the media. Getting your podcast's name and web address in inky black and white will bring you more traffic and listeners. It's easier than you might think. I'm not talking about landing yourself on *The Today Show*. You can start with your local media. If your story is newsworthy and you write a good press release, you'll get the attention you deserve.

HOW TO WRITE AN EYE-POPPING PRESS RELEASE

There is an established format for press releases that you should follow. If your release can be printed as is, without any changes, you have done a good job putting it together. It should be brief, interesting and confined to facts, but still provide the essential details of your story.

This is the basic format for a press release. The items in the brackets [ ] are information that you fill in.

FOR IMMEDIATE RELEASE

This is Where You Type Your Headline That Will Grab Their Attention in Bold
[CITY, STATE] - [DATE] - Your first paragraph should be enticing, factual and objective.

Write the rest of your story in the body. Answer who, what, where, when, why and how. The body consists of a few short paragraphs.

About [PODCAST or PODCASTER]: Include some background about yourself or your podcast, depending upon, the subject of the release.

For more information:

[NAME]

[ADDRESS]

[PHONE]

[FAX]

[WEB SITE]

[EMAIL]

###

At the top, type FOR IMMEDIATE RELEASE in all caps. Then you have the most important part of the release—your headline. If the headline doesn't catch a journalist's attention, your release won't get any further than the garbage. You have about two seconds to pique their curiosity and compel them to read on. Print the headline in bold.

Next, begin the body of your release with the date and location that the press release is coming from. The first paragraph is also very important. It must continue to entice the reader with factual, objective and interesting information. If it comes across as a sales pitch, the rest will be ignored. This paragraph needs to answer the questions who, what, where, when, why and how.

After reading the first paragraph, an editor should know what the press release is about. The headline and first paragraph tell the story. The rest of the release provides the important details that support the story. You write the body using a style called the inverted pyramid. The most important facts appear at the top of the release and the rest is written in descending order of importance. In other words, the last paragraph contains the least important information.

Below the body you can include an "about" section that gives background about your podcast. This could include how long the podcast has been around, how often it is released, how many listeners you have and any important milestones or achievements you have attained. Below that, print your contact information including your name, street address, phone, fax, web address and email. Make it clear and easy to contact you for a follow-up. Indicate the end of your press release with three # symbols.

A press release can be sent by email or snail mail (perhaps both, if you want to be sure to get attention). If you are sending your press release in print and it's longer than one page, you should print Page Two in the upper right-hand corner of the second page and -more- at the bottom of the first page.

NINE MORE TIPS FOR WRITING A RIPPING RELEASE

1. Don't use hype. Stick to the facts. Don't color the copy with superlatives like "the greatest" or "the best" and other terms of opinion. Avoid fluffy adjectives. The tone should be neutral.

2. Be succinct. Use only as many words as you need to tell the story. A good release is about 500 words long.

3. Don't use jargon. This is important with technology like podcasting. Don't use a bunch of "geek speak" that the general public won't understand.

4. Use statistics to support your story, if you have them. Statistics make a good story, and journalists like to use them.

5. Use short sentences and paragraphs to make the release easy to read. Think about how most news stories are written.

6. Make it clear who should care about the story, and why.

7. Incorporate real-life examples or a human interest story into your release. The media like these kinds of stories.

8. Use quotes that support the story. Quotes from outside sources are powerful for strengthening your release. Depending on the subject of the release, it could even contain a quote from you.

9. Don't make claims that you can't prove.

APPROPRIATE RECIPIENTS OF PRESS RELEASES

There are several places to which you can send a press release:

- TV News
- Newspapers
- Community Papers
- Trade Journals
- Radio Shows
- Television Talk Shows
- Magazines

Look in the mastheads of newspapers and magazines for editor or reporter contact info. You can also check the media outlet's web site for press release submission information. Call them and ask for the name and contact info for the section related to your topic (or at the very least, the technology editor/reporter, since podcasting is a new technology). It's best to get the name of the exact person who handles stories like yours. Don't expect it to be forwarded to the right person.

Here are some tips for contacting the press:

1. Keep it short. Don't waste their time.
2. Check your grammar and spelling.
3. Send it to targeted media contacts. Don't shoot your release to just anybody.
4. Address it to a specific person. Also, send it to the right department (e.g., technology, special interest, etc.). Find out if they prefer mail, email or fax.
5. Send snail mail in addition to email. Sending a letter takes extra effort and will help you stand out.
6. Show you know something about the media outlet and that you have personal interest in the publication or media outlet.
7. Explain why their audience will care about your story.
8. Follow up.

I suggest building up your own database of press that you send releases to on a regular basis. There are also numerous online press release outlets. Some are services that charge to submit your release to relevant media outlets. Some sites post your release for free. Here are some free PR web sites that I like to post to:

- PRWeb.com
- PR.com
- PRFree.com
- i-Newswire.com
- SBWire.com
- TheOpenPress.com
- Free-Press-Release.com
- PRLeap.com
- WebWire.com

WHEN TO SEND YOUR RELEASE

Newspapers and TV media can respond very quickly to your release and get the story out in as little as a day or two, sometimes even the same day. On the other hand, if your story revolves around a special event or a holiday, send the release at least a couple of weeks in advance. Magazines finish their content at least two months before an issue is released. I recently wrote and submitted an article for a magazine four months before the publishing date. Depending on the type of media and circumstances, plan to send out your release far enough in advance.

Keep in mind that you can send out a press release anytime something newsworthy comes along. Send them out on a regular basis. This is not just a one-shot strategy.

BUILDING YOUR CRED

The credibility factor that you gain from press is extremely important. You can't buy that kind of prestige, at least not easily. It takes years and huge marketing budgets to build up the amount of credibility that the right news story can give you in a matter of days. When you do get press, be sure to milk your newfound credibility for what it's worth. Have a page for press quotes on your site, or even include some on your home page. Not only will this build your prestige with listeners, you'll also be more likely to attract more press if they see you've already generated media buzz in the past.

The credibility factor that you gain from press is extremely important. You can't buy that kind of prestige.

LEVERAGING YOUR POSITION IN THE MEDIA

By starting a podcast, you have joined the media. In many ways, you are now a member of the press. This alone gains you some credibility. Use it to find newsworthy opportunities. Go out and find that key interview, get access to inside information and put yourself in a position to get noticed.

If there is a trade show for your niche, this is a great place to do this. Let the organizers know that you have a podcast (you may need to call it an Internet radio show for them to understand). See if you can get a press pass. Walk around the show and interview people. Trade shows are great places to find an inside scoop. If you break an interesting story, other media outlets will take notice.

You can also use your position in the press to land important interviews. Who could you interview that would attract attention? The music podcast *75 Minutes* (75minutes.com) attracted a lot of attention and listeners when it landed the first ever interview with the founder of digital music startup, Tunecore. It was able to use its position as a prominent music podcast to arrange the interview. The buzz around the interview boosted their subscriber base by about twenty percent.

THE HIDDEN BENEFIT

There's another benefit to posting your press release online, even if a media outlet doesn't pick it up. Many online press release sites include a link back to your site with the release. Not only can this draw direct web traffic, it also provides another inbound link for your off-page search engine optimization efforts.

MORE ON SELLING YOUR MESSAGE TO THE MEDIA

Spending regular effort getting press coverage can pay off in the long run by bringing more listeners and big opportunities to your podcast. If you want to get really serious with your press release campaigns, then I suggest reading *The Confessions of an Ink-Stained Wretch: An Insider's Secrets to Getting Press* by John F. Persinos. John is a Larstan colleague and editor of the book you're now reading. He's also a long-time veteran of the media, with extensive experience on newspapers, magazines, newsletters and Capitol Hill. To order his book, go to: www.inkstainedconfessions.com.

As John explains in his informative and entertaining book, the best kind of promotion is getting exposure in the press. It's free, gets seen by a lot of people and gives you more credibility. The press is always looking for interesting news. If you have a newsworthy story to tell, write up a press release—and get your message out there!

SUMMARY

Press exposure is a powerful way to promote your podcast. It's credible, far-reaching and free. The media are always looking for new and interesting content. Find or create a newsworthy angle about your podcast, then contact the press and tell them about it. You do this by sending a press release.

A press release is a concise summary of your newsworthy story. It contains the most relevant information with the most important facts first. Send regular press releases to carefully chosen contacts in the media who handle your topic in the press. You can also post it to press release sites such as *PRWeb.com*. With the right story and some perseverance, you can land some media exposure, bringing you more traffic and credibility.

> **Multimedia Tutorials at PodcastingUniversity.org**
>
> For more help with the topics covered in this chapter, please visit: www.PodcastingUniversity.org/pyp/chapter7
>
> You'll find multimedia tutorials on:
>
> - How to find press outlets to send your releases to
>
> As well as further resources such as:
>
> - Example press releases
> - Press release templates
> - A list of recommended professional press release writing services
>
> ...and more!

Converting Listeners into Raving Fans

BUILDING A RELATIONSHIP WITH YOUR LISTENERS

One of the most alluring aspects of podcasting is that your voice goes out to a potentially worldwide audience. Moreover, you have a direct connection to your audience. There's no TV or radio network serving as an intermediary between you and them. You produce a show and release it directly to your audience. This model represents a shift in how a medium is created and distributed. It's the masses talking to the masses, not just the masses being spoon-fed limited content from a select few.

This direct connection facilitates interaction with your listeners. They hear your voice, relate to what you're saying and a relationship develops. They start talking back! Unlike most mainstream media, the communication flows both ways. You get feedback, questions and praise directly from your listeners. Emails come in. Voice comments are submitted. Comments appear on your blog.

This is the nature of social media, such as podcasting. As a podcaster, it's extremely important to encourage dialogue and cultivate this relationship with your listeners. To truly build your audience, you must keep them listening and loyal. Any savvy businessperson will tell you that it's easier to keep a current customer than to convert a new one. The same applies to your listeners, whether your podcast is for business, or not.

. . . you don't just want listeners—you want raving fans.

Besides, you don't just want listeners—you want raving fans. You want them to become "evangelizers" for your show. Word-of-mouth advertising from a loyal listener is the best marketing you can get. Regular contact and interaction with your listeners helps transition them into raving fans.

Build a relationship with your audience and develop loyal fans by providing ways for them to convey comments, offer feedback or speak whatever else is on their mind. The amount of feedback that you get will increase as your audience gets bigger and develops more of a connection with you.

Also, encourage your listeners to interact with each other. This sense of community and "water cooler talk" helps keep them excited about your show. Let's look at the most common methods of communicating with your listeners.

EMAIL FEEDBACK

Email has become a universal means of communication on the Internet. Create an email address just for your podcast. Personally, I think it looks best to have an email that is from your own website (e.g., talk@yourwebaddress.com). It comes across as more professional and helps brand your site and show.

If you use a web email service like GMail, I suggest obtaining an address such as nameofpodcast@gmail.com. Whatever email address you choose, remember that you'll be giving it out on your podcast. It should be easy for people to spell and remember just by hearing it on your show.

VOICE COMMENTS

In as much as podcasting is an audio medium, it makes sense to solicit audio comments from your listeners. Voice comments serve as great show content. They add variety and your listeners will love hearing their voice. The prospect of having their thoughts shared on the show will encourage people to comment.

Keep in mind that most listeners won't have the means or know-how to record a high quality audio to send to you. A podcaster should offer easy means for anyone to spontaneously submit audio feedback. There are a few ways to do this. The most obvious is to use a voice message call-in line. Here are a few things to consider if you go this route:

- Is the phone number easy for people to remember?
- Is it the call toll-free for your listeners? This will cost you more, but encourages more listeners to call.
- If you have a long-distance phone number it will cost less for you, but it might discourage others from calling.
- Do you have international listeners? Will it work for them as well? Most toll-free numbers don't work if someone is calling from outside of your country. In this case, a regular phone number works best instead of, or in addition to, a toll-free number.
- Is it easy to get the voice message to your computer for use in your podcast? Some voice messaging services will send you a digital audio file of the message.

Here are three recommended solutions for allowing your listeners to submit voice comments:

K7.net

A lot of podcasters in the United States use K7.net for their voicemail. This is a free service for you, but the phone number is not toll-free for your listeners. You choose an available number with a 206 area code in Seattle, Washington. When a listener leaves a message, an audio file (in .wav format) is emailed to you, making it easy to use in your podcast.

Pros:
- Free
- Message is emailed to you as an audio file
- International listeners can call it

Cons:
- Not toll free for listeners
- Phone numbers all have a 206 area code (from the Seattle area)
- Limited choice of phone numbers
- Probably only a good solution for those who have most of their listeners in the U.S.

Skype

Skype is a free program for making calls over the Internet. You can download it at `skype.com`. It has become very popular among podcasters. The calls over the Internet are also free. You can add voicemail to your Skype account for a small fee. Listeners can leave you a message if they have your Skype ID, and call you from another computer with Skype installed.

You also can buy an inexpensive SkypeIn number. This is a phone number that, when called, connects to your Skype account and will ring you if you're online, or allow the caller to leave a message if you're not. SkypeIn numbers are available in several countries. You can even buy a number for a country other than the one where you live.

Pros:
- Free for Skype users to call and leave a message over the Internet
- Skype voicemails are saved to your hard drive, making them easy to use in your show

Cons:
- To get a phone number costs money, although not very much
- Unless you purchase a SkypeIn phone number, your listeners also must have Skype to call you

Toll-Free Voicemail

If your listeners are all in your own country, you can consider getting a toll-free voicemail to make it free for your listeners. There are numerous toll-free voicemail services, with prices and features that are constantly changing. They also vary by country. If you're in the U.S., I recommend looking at `Kall8.com`, which is related to K7.net (mentioned above).

Pros:
- Free to your listeners, if they're in the same country
- Toll-free might encourage more listeners to call, because it's free for them

Cons:

- There is a charge to you for every minute used on a call to the number
- The toll-free voicemail service may not send you an audio file to use in your podcast
- International listeners will probably not be able to call the number

BLOG COMMENTS

If your podcast is published to a blog, it should already be set up to accept comments for each post. Most blog programs offer this feature. There's probably a comments link or form underneath each blog post. This is where site visitors can post their own thoughts. It's also a great place to get feedback from your listeners. Remind your listeners that they can post comments under the post for a specific episode.

3 Comments »

Andrew Thomas said,
March 28, 2006 at 3:30 pm · Edit

I just wanted to thank you for your podcast program. I only recently started my online business and I was searching everywhere for information that was helpful and not all hype. In other words I was looking for something related to the truth as to how much work was actually involved.
I discovered your podcast and it has been very helpful.

Thanks
Andrew Thomas

If you're worried about getting inappropriate comments, you should be able to set up your blog to not post a new comment until you clear it. Take a look at your blog instructions for more information on how to do this. This feature is usually called comment moderation.

ENCOURAGING THE CONVERSATION

Make it easy for your audience to communicate with you and each other. Put your contact info on every page of your site. Make it obvious how your listeners can reach you. Have a *Contact Us* page on your site. Mention your contact info on every episode of your podcast.

Give your listeners options. Some people prefer calling. Others like email. You should offer a variety of methods for sending feedback. Let your audience decide which they prefer.

It also helps to dish out some acknowledgment and appreciation on your show when listeners submit comments. The power of the "shout out" never ceases to amaze me. Everyone loves a little recognition. Even my family and friends who know me enjoy hearing me mention their names on the podcast.

If you read emails or play audio comments on your show, mention the name of the person who commented. People love to hear their name "on air." Your listeners will love it when they feel as if they have contributed to, and made a mark on, the podcast. Also, thank your listeners when they comment. Appreciation goes a long way.

INTERACTING WITH YOUR AUDIENCE

Not only should your podcast be a "conversation" with your audience, it should also be interactive. Give your listeners ways to participate in the show and interact with you. Your listeners will become loyal fans as they participate. It gives them a sense of ownership in the content. It builds a sense of community.

Not only should your podcast be a "conversation" with your audience, it should also be interactive.

Here are some ideas for making your podcast an interactive experience:

- Ask your listeners for their opinion

- Ask your listeners for a favor
- Hold a contest
- Ask a specific question and solicit answers
- Invite users to submit a podcast ID for the show (e.g., "Hi. This is Bob Smith and you're listening to *NameOfPodcast.*"
- Ask your listeners to vote on something, such as the subject of an episode
- Conduct a poll or survey and share the results on the show

MESSAGE BOARDS

You also can consider adding a forum to your site, for your audience to communicate with you and with each other. Two examples of podcasts that effectively use message boards to build community are *75 Minutes* (www.75minutes.com) and *Dailysonic* (www.dailysonic.com).

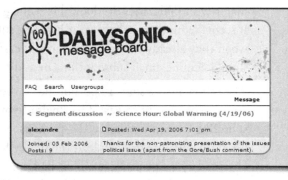

Mike, host of *75 Minutes,* explains how having a message board on their site has built a sense of community. "It creates two-way communication. I get continual feedback that helps me to improve the show. In addition, two of our forum participants now regularly research and contribute music for the podcast. They were fans and now they get to make it happen." Adam, of *Dailysonic,* points out another advantage of having a forum. "In addition to creating community, a message board produces regular text content on our site. This provides great fodder for the search engines to index, bringing us more traffic. It also brings visitors back to the site, again and again. Repeat traffic increases how many times our banner advertisements are seen, bringing in more money."

Check with your web host about adding a message board to your site. Some hosts offer an easy way to install a forum or will even do it for you. If you're comfortable installing one yourself, or willing to hire a web programmer to do so, I recommend phpBB (phpbb.com). This is a popular and free forum application. If you use Worpress to run your blog, you can take a look at XDForum (`xdweb.net`). This is a Wordpress plugin that adds a forum to your blog.

There are also several free message board services that will host a forum for you, although this means it is not on your own site. A Google search for *message board service* or *forum service* will point you in the right direction. I can't recommend one since I haven't used any of them myself.

THE MOST IMPORTANT, AND OFTEN OVERLOOKED, COMMUNICATION STRATEGY

The single most important measure that podcasters can take to communicate with their audience is building an email list of their listeners. The majority of podcasters overlook this strategy, and I can understand why. It seems redundant to have your listeners subscribe to an email list when they already subscribe to your podcast, but every podcaster should acquire email subscriptions in addition to podcast subscriptions.

The following are some important facts, though they may not be what you expect or want to hear. Only half of your listeners will actually subscribe to your podcast feed—perhaps fewer. The others will simply listen on your site or download the file by hand. This behavior has been observed by many podcasters. I've had episodes that were listened to by as many as four times the number of people I have as subscribers. That's a lot of site visitors to let slip away without having a way to follow up with them.

Right now, you might be screaming: "But that's the power of a podcast feed! Content just comes to me automatically! Why don't they all subscribe if they like it?!" Well, consider this: Several years ago, not everyone understood, or used, email despite the fact that it was faster and more convenient than snail mail. It took time, but now just about everyone has an email address.

Likewise, feed syndication on the Internet is a relatively new technology. It will take time before everyone understands and adopts it. In a few years, the majority of Internet users will have their favorite feed reader and handful of content subscriptions. Until then, we have to work with the realities of podcast consumer behavior.

You can't expect every listener to subscribe to the podcast feed. Some people will find your web site, listen to your show, like it, maybe book mark the site and think they'll check back periodically for new episodes. But then they'll get busy and forget to come back — unless you remind them.

I collect as many email addresses as possible from listeners and site visitors. If someone gives you an email address, they're essentially raising their hand and saying, "I like what you're offering and I'd like more of it." This kind of targeted list is an extremely valuable asset. A targeted list takes action when you communicate with them. It is a powerful tool for building listener loyalty, attracting sponsors, making money and promoting your podcast.

I send out an email reminder to my list every time I release a new episode. I immediately see a nice spike in traffic. It doesn't cost me anything to send out an email. It's like creating traffic from thin air.

To successfully grow your audience, make money with your podcast or achieve whatever other goals you may have as a podcaster, you need to collect email addresses on your site. Then contact these people on a regular basis.

You also can add a regular newsletter or e-zine to your list, in addition to show announcements. It could include articles or other text content that supplements your podcast. Having an email list provides another way to maintain regular contact with your listeners. It maintains you're in the forefront of their minds. It keeps them coming back to listen, again and again.

I'm a musician. During years of would-be rock star pursuits, I played a lot of live shows with several different bands. We always collected email addresses at our gigs and on our web site. This was integral to growing our fan base and creating buzz.

If we didn't keep in touch with our fans, our show attendance would start to dip. Your audience needs to hear from you on a regular basis or they'll start to forget about you and your podcast. There may be times when you want to contact your listeners without producing and sending out an episode. Email is perfect for this kind of contact.

There is one more key advantage to collecting email addresses. If you tell a potential sponsor that you have a thousand email addresses, it will entice them even more than just having a thousand feed subscriptions. One thousand people who have chosen to give you their email address can impress your potential sponsors. You won't need to share your email list with them, but the size of your list, and the prospect of also placing an ad in your emails, will only help to entice them.

THE DAY I ALMOST LOST ALL MY PODCAST SUBSCRIBERS

The time I almost lost every *Internet Business Mastery* subscriber offers another poignant reason why it's important to have multiple ways to reach your listeners. Over a two-week period we had noticed our subscriber stats were plummeting into the basement. How could this be? Did we say something wrong? Did we tell a bad joke? Sure, listeners come and go, but this just didn't make any sense.

We finally figured out that a bug in one of the major podcatchers had switched the majority of our subscribers over to a podcast feed address that was invalid. The listeners were not getting our updates. We couldn't speak with our subscribers because the podcatcher had stopped downloading new episodes.

The worst part was that our feed subscribers had no way of knowing it — and we had no other way of telling them. At the time, we hadn't started collecting emails yet. Fortunately I found a creative, albeit rather technical, way to fix the problem. I was able to switch everyone back to the correct address. Still, I was sweating it for a few days. I almost lost months of promotion and time spent building my audience. If I'd had an email list, I would have had a fail-safe in a situation like this. RSS is a great technology that allows podcast feeds, but it has its frailties and drawbacks. Strengthen your position by building an email list.

LIST BUILDING MASTERY

There are several steps you can take to increase the percentage of site visitors that subscribe to your email list. Here are 11 of my best email list-building tips:

1. Make the email sign-up form very prominent on your home page. I like to have a strong headline that asks visitors to sign up. On podcastingunderground.com, I have a bright red headline in a handwritten font. It's right at the top with an arrow pointing to the sign up form. It's impossible for someone not to see it.

   Sign up for my podcasting tips ezine and get a a free audio tip on how to get more listeners from the podcast directories.

2. Put an email list subscription form on every page of your site. It should be prominent and obvious. If you're using a blog for your podcast, you probably have a sidebar on every page. This is a great place to put it. It's usually at the top of my sidebars.

3. Tell people exactly what to expect from your email newsletter. What kind of content or updates will you send them? How often? This helps them feel more comfortable about giving their information. Give them two or three bullet points stating what benefits they'll get for signing up. On PodcastingUnderground.com, I make it clear that they'll get exclusive tips and commentary to help them with their podcast.

4. I ask people to *sign up* for my email list and *subscribe* to my podcast. Using two different verbs helps make it clear that they're two different entities to subscribe to.

   Free Ezine Sign-Up

   It's free. Subscribe today and YOU get:

   - My free audio tip on how to get more listeners from the podcast directories.
   - Exclusive tips for creating, publishing and promoting your podcast
   - News and articles on the latest breakthroughs in the podcasting industry

   Enter Your First Name

   Enter Your Primary Email

   Yes Subscribe Me

5. Come up with a name for your email newsletter. At the very least, you can call it the *Name of Podcast Email Newsletter or E-zine.*

6. Give your site visitors a reason to subscribe. Offer them an exclusive show for subscribers only, or give them access to other special content as a gift for subscribing.

   It's best to offer access to the exclusive content in an email after they subscribe. This way they have to give you a real email address to receive your special content. If you offer the right incentive, it's an incredibly powerful way of converting more email sign ups.

   For my *Podcasting Underground* list I offer an exclusive podcast promotion tip to those who sign up. For *Internet Business Mastery*, we offer a video tutorial. It should be something that your site visitors will be itching to get their hands on.

7. Regularly mention your email list on your podcast, during every episode, if you can. This is especially important if you start your email list after you already have a number of listeners and subscribers. You want them to sign up for the email list, as well. In addition, you'll have a lot of listeners who find, and subscribe to, your podcast without ever actually visiting your site. Inform them about the email list in the show and ask them to visit your site to subscribe. Be sure to mention the incentive they get for signing up.

8. Under your signup form include a statement, such as *"Your information will never be shared. I will never send you spam. You can read my Privacy Policy here."*

   Having a strong "no spam" statement and an obvious link to your privacy policy helps visitors feel more comfortable about giving up their email address. Here is our privacy policy for *Internet Business Mastery:*

Internet Business Mastery Privacy Policy

Your privacy is important to us. On this site you can buy products & sign up for our e-newsletter. To help you make decisions about the information you provide anywhere on this site, this notice has been provided to outline our practices.

We use secure hosting accounts and other security measures to protect our database and any information provided.

Any email you receive from this site will contain the option to unsubscribe at the end of the email. You can unsubscribe at any time. When you order a product, the information you provide will only be provided to outside parties if it is necessary to complete and deliver the order. Your information will never be shared or disclosed to other parties for any other reason.

Non-identifying information may be used to improve the site or shared with advertisers. For instance, information that is collected regarding traffic to the site or specific pages may be shared, but this will never include any identifying information.

9. The more information you ask for, the better. Sometimes I only ask for first name and email, other times I provide an entire survey to fill out. The amount of info you request will depend on your goals. If you're podcasting for business reasons, then a full name and mailing address would also be useful.

The more info you ask for, the more reluctant visitors will be to sign up, but the more targeted the list will be. You know that someone is really interested in what you have if they'll give you all their info. I've posted sites where visitors were required to take a relatively lengthy survey to sign up for my email list. The response was still considerable because we gave them valuable information and a powerful incentive for signing up. Decide what you're comfortable with and what is appropriate for your audience and goals.

10. In your email sign-up form, ask for the primary email. A lot of people have more than one email address. Sometimes just asking for the primary email will make the difference in getting the best address from them.

11. Always allow email subscribers to automatically unsubscribe from your email list. This is just good business practice—and it might be the law, depending on where you live.

MANAGING YOUR EMAIL LIST

Unless you want to go crazy, you need an automatic way to send emails out, and for people to subscribe and unsubscribe to the list. Here are three recommended solutions for managing your email list:

Feedblitz

Feedblitz (`feedblitz.com`) is a service that automatically sends reminders to your list of new blog/podcast posts. It gives you a simple form to place on your web site that lets your site visitors sign up to receive regular updates from your blog/podcast. It's a very simple and hands-off solution, if that is all you need.

The basic service is free, but for a small monthly fee you can upgrade your account and get additional features. Upgrading your account allows you to send out messages in addition to the blog/podcast update announcements. In addition, you can choose to have the email come from you, rather than Feedblitz. This allows people to reply to you, and makes it more likely for them to open the email.

Google or Yahoo Groups

Google and Yahoo both offer free services for starting a private or public email group. They can be found at `groups.google.com` and `groups.yahoo.com`, respectively. Starting a group with either of these services is simple. You'll need a free Google or Yahoo ID, depending on which service you use. Be sure to change the settings so that only you, the moderator, can send out messages. Otherwise, anyone can post an email to the group. You can place a simple form on your web site to allow your visitors to sign up for the list.

GetResponse

If you want an advanced and full-featured solution for managing your email list, I recommend GetResponse (`getresponse.com`). It provides a gamut of features, including customizable sign-up forms, importing/ exporting your list and sending out an automatic series of emails to new subscribers. This is the most expensive solution, but well worth it if you have serious long-term goals for your podcast and email list.

SUMMARY

Podcasting allows you to have a direct connection with your audience. It's important to encourage your audience to give feedback and participate in the show. This sense of community will turn listeners into fans who spread the word about your podcast. It's easier to keep your current listeners than to find new ones.

Offer several ways for your audience to communicate with you, such as email, comments on your blog, a message board and a voicemail call-in line. Ask for feedback to encourage interaction. Frequently mention how listeners can send in their comments. Use your listeners comments in the show and thank them for their participation. This will motivate your audience to participate more and give them a sense of ownership to the show.

It's also important to collect email addresses from your audience. Building an email list gives you another way to contact your audience and keep them coming back for more. Offer an incentive to encourage your listeners to sign up for your email updates. Feedblitz, Yahoo Groups, Google Groups and GetResponse are all services that can help you manage your email list.

Multimedia Tutorials at PodcastingUniversity.org

For more help with the topics covered in this chapter, please visit: www.PodcastingUniversity.org/pyp/chapter8

You'll find multimedia tutorials on:

- Starting and managing an email list
- Converting site visitors into email list subscribers
- Setting up a voicemail service for your podcast
- Adding a forum to your website

As well as further resources such as:

- A list of additional voicemail services
- A list of additional interactive features for your website
- Case studies on succesful audience interaction initiatives

...and more!

Getting the Most from Your Promotion

THE KEY TO CONTINUAL MARKETING SUCCESS

One of my prime directives in marketing is to track, track, track. If you don't follow the growth of your audience, how do you know if you're marketing is working, or if you're just wasting your time? I imagine if you're promoting your podcast, it's because you want to see your audience grow. To do this, you need to keep an eye on some web statistics.

Don't let me scare you off with talk of statistics. It was one of my least favorite college classes, too. I'll keep the numbers discussion as easy and streamlined as I can. I assure you, it's really exciting when you see people flocking to your show. The ego gratification is very satisfying.

Here's the simple three-step formula for continually growing your audience:

1. Regularly apply the promotion ideas and tips in this book
2. Watch your statistics to see what is working best for your show
3. Do more of what is working best

Now, I have some good and bad news. The bad news is that tracking podcasting statistics is an imperfect science, at best. The good news is that you can still keep tabs on the growth of your audience by watching relative trends in the numbers. In this chapter, we're going to look at four sets of statistics:

1. The general trend of your audience growth based on downloads, subscribers stats and bandwidth
2. How many visitors come to your site
3. Where the traffic is coming from
4. Which keywords are bringing traffic from the search engines

These statistics will tell you a valuable story about your podcast. They'll give you a sense for what kind of mileage you're getting from your marketing. I'll also show you how to eavesdrop on what people are saying about your show out in cyberspace. This will help you get a feel for the buzz you're generating.

AN IMPERFECT SCIENCE (OR A THEORY OF RELATIVITY)

Measuring the size of your audience is riddled with challenges. There's still a lot of guesswork and inflated figures being tossed around by podcasters and industry analysts (if we can even claim to have analysts, yet). Think about magazines, newspapers, television and radio. They have no way of knowing exactly how many people read an issue, watch a show, or tune in during the commute. They've had to develop methods for approximating their numbers and watching trends.

Ideally the size of your audience is a measurement of how many people currently download, and listen, to each episode. Unfortunately, there's really no way to know how many people actually listen to the podcast once the file is downloaded—aside from polling your listeners.

The next best solution is to track the number of complete downloads of each episode by a unique listener (meaning they have not downloaded the file before). However, this is easier said than done. It involves the cost and effort of installing the right software on your web host, and it's still just an approximation in the end.

For now, we'll rely on numbers that are more readily available and, while not ideal, still give you a feel for how fast you're gaining listeners. By watching the relative growth of your audience over time, you'll see when you get a significant spike in listeners. You'll see what works best for attracting new listeners and where they're coming from. You'll also determine which of your episodes get more listeners than the others. The relative growth of your audience can be tracked by watching the following five statistics:

1. The number of unique downloads of a podcast file from the feed
2. The number of unique downloads of a podcast by someone clicking a link on your site
3. The number of unique people who regularly check your feed for new episodes (also called subscribers)
4. The number of hits to a given podcast file (I'll elaborate on the difference between a hit and a download shortly)
5. The amount of bandwidth used for downloads of a given episode

Your audience consists of two kinds of listeners, those that download the show directly and those who download episodes through the feed with an aggregator. The latter are referred to as subscribers. Your subscribers can be measured one of two ways — by looking at the number of unique aggregators that access your podcast feed on a regular basis, taking into account multiple accesses from the same aggregator and computer, or by counting the number of downloads that occur from the feed.

Many podcasters have noticed that as many as half of their file downloads occur from someone clicking a link on their site.

As much as we want to believe that podcasting is all about the feed technology, some people are still listening the old-fashioned way, by downloading or streaming it from your site. They don't all subscribe to the feed to grab new episodes. Many podcasters have noticed that as many as half of their file downloads occur from someone clicking a link on their site.

In addition to download and subscriber stats, you can also watch the number of hits to a given podcast file and the overall bandwidth transfer resulting from a given episode. A hit occurs when a file is accessed on your web site. When someone downloads all, or part of, an mp3 file, it registers as a hit in your web logs.

Bandwidth is a measure of how much data is being transferred to, and from, your site. A 20 MB file uses up 20 MB of bandwidth each time it is downloaded. Most of your bandwidth usage will be from downloads of your podcast files, which are much larger and take more bandwidth than web pages and picture files.

There are several tools that you can use to measure these numbers. I'll go over the most common stat tools. The following chart lists what each of them measures:

Stats Platform	Unique Feed Downloads	Unique Feed Subscribers	Unique Web Click Downloads	# of Hits to a File	Bandwidth Use per File
Libsyn's Stats	Yes	Yes	Yes	Yes	No
AWStats	No	No	No	Yes	Yes
FeedBurner	Yes (pro version)	Yes	No	No	No

Libsyn (www.libsyn.com) is a popular podcast hosting service. It provides everything you need to start and maintain a podcast, including unmetered bandwidth and a number of useful statistics. Most web hosts provide AWStats with your hosting. AWStats tracks several web site stats. If your host doesn't provide AWStats, you can ask if they'll install it, or get it yourself for free at awstats.sourceforge.net. FeedBurner (www.feedburner.com) is a free service that measures your feed subscribers, among other things.

HOW TO MEASURE THE GROWTH OF YOUR AUDIENCE

Most statistics software packages measure the number of hits to each file on your web site, including your audio or video files. Looking at the number of hits to a podcast file for a given episode gives you a feel for the size of your audience.

Keep in mind, the number of hits will be higher than the actual number of people who download and listen to your show. The reason is that even a partial download registers as a hit. You can also get multiple hits during a single complete download. Another common problem is that the same listener might download an episode more than once on different computers, or with different aggregators, leading to several hits from one person.

But remember, we're looking for relative numbers right now. If you see this number going up from episode to episode, it's safe to assume that your audience is growing. If you have an episode in a given month that gets a lot more hits than the others, there's something about that show that attracted more listeners. These are the kinds of trends that you want to watch for and think about.

Let's take a look at some of the most common web hosts and statistics programs, to show you specifically how to keep an eye on these statistics.

Libsyn

The following figure is an example of the statistics panel from an episode posted to the Libsyn demo account:

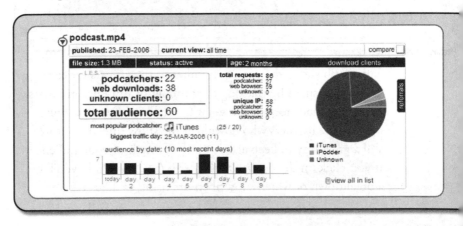

To access your statistics in Libsyn, log in to your account and click the *Stats* tab. You'll see a chart like the one on the previous page listed for each of your episodes. In the upper left-hand corner, you have a breakdown of your audience. Next to *podcatchers* is a measurement of how many unique individuals are downloading your show through the feed. *Web downloads* is a measurement of how many times the file was downloaded directly from your site. *Unknown clients* measures the number of accesses to the file that could not be identified. The sum of these three numbers equals the total size of your audience. The chart in the upper right-hand corner shows you what podcatchers and aggregators are being used to download your podcast.

FeedBurner

FeedBurner provides some very useful statistics as part of its service. If you already have a FeedBurner account, you can access the statistics by logging in and selecting the name of the show whose stats you want to see. You'll see a graph like the one in the figure below:

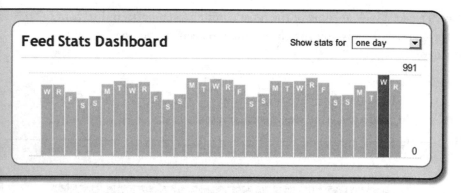

The graph shows the average number of subscribers for each day. This is measured by tracking the number of unique computers that access your feed on a regular basis. These numbers don't include the listeners who download the show directly, but it's still a great way to keep an eye on the growth of your audience. If you click on the *See live subscriber information* link, you'll get a breakdown of which subscribers are using each aggregator.

As you can see in this chart the vast majority of subscribers use iTunes.

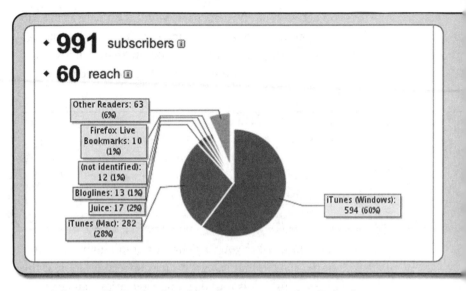

The FeedBurner subscriber statistic is one that I check on a regular basis to get a feel for how many people are listening and how fast my audience is growing. If you pay for the pro stats from FeedBurner, you also get a breakdown of how many downloads each episode gets through the feed.

If you already have an established podcast, but want to start using FeedBurner for stats, remember there are a couple of issues to keep in mind that I covered in the Introduction.

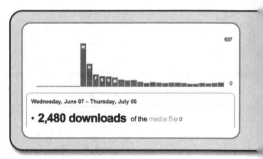

AWStats

AWStats is a very common web statistics program that is included with most web hosting accounts. Refer to your web host support to see if they have it installed for your account and how to access the stats page. Your web host may also provide a stat program called Webalizer that tracks similar things.

When you access your AWStats page, you'll see a date at the top indicating when the stats were last updated. You can also select which month's stats you want to view. Below that, you'll see a variety of links that take you down the page to different sets of numbers:

When:	Monthly history Days of month Days of week Hours
Who:	Countries Full list Hosts Full list Last visit Unresolved IP Address Robots/Spiders visitors Full list Last visit
Navigation:	Visits duration File type Viewed Full list Entry Exit Operating Systems Versions Unknown Browsers Versions Unknown
Referers:	Origin Refering search engines Refering sites Search Search Keyphrases Search Keywords
Others:	Miscellaneous HTTP Status codes Pages not found

Each of these links takes you to a chart or graph giving you an analysis of the stats in that category. First, let's take a look at the *Viewed* pages. This link is found in the Navigation category. When you click on this link you'll be taken to a chart that looks like the figure below:

Pages-URL (Top 10)	-	Full list -	
95 different pages-url		Viewed	Average size
/mp3s/episode03		3133	19.23 MB
/mp3s/episode04		2742	18.41 MB
/mp3s/episode06		2521	14.29 MB
/mp3s/episode05		2496	17.70 MB

This chart gives you the 10 most accessed pages or files on your web site. For a podcast, you should see several audio files listed here. To get the entire list, click on the *Full List* link. The number that is particularly interesting here is in the *Viewed* column.

This is the number of hits the file has received. This number will be higher than the actual number of downloads or listens the file received, because a hit may not have resulted in a full download and a full download could require multiple hits.

However, this does give you a relative idea of which episodes are most popular. If these numbers are getting higher with each episode, then more people are "tuning in."

Don't forget, you're only looking at the numbers for the current month. If you want to know the cumulative number of hits a podcast file has received, you'll need to also add together this number from each of the previous months that the episode was available.

Let's take a look at some other interesting numbers that AWStats provides. Back at the top, click on the *Monthly History* link.

Month	Unique visitors	Number of visits	Pages	Hits	Bandwidth
Jan 2006	5331	10623	26933	41141	301.91 GB
Feb 2006	5738	10726	27142	43953	310.24 GB
Mar 2006	6126	11932	27748	40084	338.71 GB
Apr 2006	4532	9874	16588	33951	224.07 GB

This chart gives you a rundown of the visits and bandwidth for your site, by month. These numbers provide another good snapshot of the overall growth of your audience. The *Unique Visits* column indicates the number of unique visitors your site has received that month, filtering out duplicate visits from someone who has already accessed your site that month. The *Number of Visits* column is the total visits including return visits by the same person.

Bandwidth is the total amount of data being transferred, for all files, from your site on a monthly basis. For a podcast site, the vast majority of this bandwidth is a result of podcast file downloads. This is another relative gauge of how many people are downloading your show.

Now go back and click on the *Days of Month* link. You'll see a chart displaying the number of visits that your site received for each day of the month. I regularly watch this chart for a spike in traffic after I run a promotion, or if there is an unexpected spike, I try to determine what caused it. I look to see if someone new linked to me or if there is some other reason for an influx of visitors.

The *Robots/Spiders Visitors* link takes you to a chart displaying the search engine spiders that have visited your site this month. Some of the names you'll see here include MSNBot, Googlebot and Inktomi Slurp (Yahoo's crawler).

To see where your site visitors are coming from, click on the *Referring Sites* link. This chart contains a list of web pages that are bringing you traffic. The number in the *Pages* column is a measure of how many site visitors have clicked through to your site from that page. This is a good place to look if you comment on a blog or acquire a new inbound link from a site. You'll be able to see if it results in any traffic. If you get traffic from a site, it's worth performing more promotion on that site, because you know it's working.

I once noticed in AWStats that I was getting traffic to *Gotham-Cast* from an Italian forum for New York enthusiasts. I decided to investigate and left a comment on the message board (in Italian, no less). This resulted in more traffic. It pays to keep an eye on your traffic and where it's coming from.

Finally, click on the *Search KeyPhrases* link at the top of the AWStats page. This chart will tell you the search phrases that are resulting in clicks to your site. If a phrase appears in this table, it means that someone searched for that phrase, your site appeared in the listings and they clicked on it. The number in the *Search* column tells you how many visits a phrase has produced.

This is a good way to keep track of your progress in search engine marketing. Are you getting clicks from the phrases you thought you would? Do you see other phrases you could target even more? Do you need to put more effort into some of your primary keyword phrases?

That's all the numbers we'll look at in AWStats, but it's worth spending some time perusing the other charts. Familiarize yourself with the numbers and what they can tell you. There's a wealth of information to be found there.

MORE TOOLS FOR TRACKING STATS

If you want to take your stat tracking even further, there are a couple other tools I have found useful. RadioTail's Ripple is a free stat tracking service for podcasters. You can grab a Ripple account at www.radiotail.com/ripple. It takes a bit of time to set up, but you'll get stats about your episode downloads and feed subscribers. I also recommend looking into RadioTail's ad technology that allows you to insert ads into mp3 downloads on the fly.

If you use Wordpress to publish your podcast, check out a fully loaded podcasting plugin called Podpress (www.mightyseek.com/podpress/). This free program offers too many features to list here, but one of the best is the statistics page that reports both the number of site and feed downloads. To top it off, Podpress lets you easily insert a media player into each blog post and reports how many times it's used to stream the episode.

WHAT KIND OF NUMBERS YOU CAN EXPECT

Despite steady growth, podcasting is still in its infancy. Combine that with the fact that podcasting is often best used to target niche audiences. You can't expect a podcast to have as many listeners or viewers as a major radio or television station. This is important to realize so you can set reasonable goals and expectations for the growth of your audience and the proliferation of your message.

How many listeners can you expect to have? Obviously this will depend on the nature of your podcast. A podcast that is launched by a major network, such as NPR or MTV, is going to have an instant listener base, while an "independent" podcaster will start from scratch.

You can see which podcasts have the most feed subscribers according to FeedBurner at www.podfeed.net/FeedBurner_rankings.asp. I should mention that this list consists only of those podcasts that have opted to make their statistics public and represents only a slice of the podcasts out there, but it offers some interesting insights. As a side note, your FeedBurner stats are private, by default. Also, keep in mind that these numbers only measure subscribers and do not include listeners who download or stream from a web site.

At the time of writing this book, the top podcast on the list is *Diggnation,* with 32,569 subscribers. But if we look at the #5 position, *English as a Second Language,* the number of subscribers has already dropped to 10,486. In the #10 slot, we have *TOEFL Podcast* (looks as if language podcasts do well), with 5,526 subscribers.

As you can see, it is currently a very small number of podcasts that can claim a subscriber base in the tens of thousands. Cruising down to the bottom of the list, we see that the podcast at #100 has 585 subscribers. I bring this up as a point of encouragement. You don't have to have thousands of subscribers to feel good about your show. You can aspire to that, but realize that the majority of podcasts right now can't claim over 1,000 subscribers.

Here's how I breakdown the average growth cycle of a podcast (I'm speaking here to indie podcasters who are starting from scratch, not big media and companies with a list of current consumers). Just by launching your podcast and telling your friends, you should be able to attract a nice handful of listeners, let's say up to 50. By submitting your podcast to the directories, you should to at least double that number quickly, and even rise above 100 subscribers. When you surpass the 200-300 mark, you're making some good progress. This is an audience to be proud of, and you're on your way.

Naturally, if you have high hopes or business aspirations for your podcast, you'll want an audience that's bigger than that — and it will come. It's just unfortunate when I hear that a podcaster wants to quit because "nobody is listening," when in actuality they have as many subscribers as any other well-established independent podcast.

So keep your expectations at a reasonable level. Be patient and work on consistent growth. There is an audience out there waiting for you. You don't have to be Ricky Gervais or Rush Limbaugh to find a niche audience that loves and raves about your show. Podcasting is still new, but it is growing fast. By positioning yourself now, you'll be ready for the upcoming growth spurts.

If you are starting a podcast for a major media outlet or a business with a large customer list, then for you it's a different story. You know your consumers and should be able to estimate how many of them will respond and listen to your show, assuming you promote it to them. By all means, market your podcast to your customer list if you have one. Tell your current listeners or viewers about it.

THEY'RE TALKING ABOUT YOU BEHIND YOUR BACK

Do you want to know what people are saying about you and your podcast? Here are some nifty tricks for eavesdropping. In the chapter on social networking sites we talked about Technorati. Technorati is a great tool for tracking what's being said about you on other blogs and podcasts. By entering your name or the name of your podcast on the search page, you'll get a list of blogs and podcasts that have mentioned you. Your search will be most effective if you place double quotes around it. This searches for the exact phrase as you've entered it. It's also useful to do a search for your web address.

To keep track of web sites that mention or link to you, use Google Alerts. Google Alerts will email you whenever a new web search or news listing shows up in Google for a given phrase. Go to `www.google.com/alerts`. Next to *Search terms,* enter your name or the name of your podcast in double quotes. Next to *Type,* select *News & Web.* Then select how often you want to receive email updates, and click the *Create Alert* button.

Another tool that I use often is PubSub's SiteStats, available at `www.pubsub.com/site_stats.php`. When you visit this page you'll be asked to enter a web address. Enter your podcast's web address and it will return a list of inbound links to it. It also creates a feed that you can subscribe to in order to get regular updates of new links.

If you shoulder all the work of attracting visitors to your web site, you may as well pave the way for them to become listeners or subscribers.

CONVERTING SITE VISITORS TO LISTENERS

If you shoulder all the work of attracting visitors to your web site, you may as well pave the way for them to become listeners or subscribers. There are several steps I follow on my podcast site to make it easy for someone to listen or subscribe:

- Include an explanation of the term "podcast"
- Make it clear how and why to subscribe
- Include a media player that allows them to quickly and easily sample your show
- Make it obvious what your feed address is
- Include links for automatically subscribing in popular aggregators, such as iTunes and Yahoo

Take a look at the header for my *GothamCast* site (www.gothamcast.com):

First, you have the description of the show that tells the visitor exactly what to expect and entices them to listen. If you click on the podcast link, it takes you to an article that defines the term "podcast."

Second, I tell them what exactly to do. They can listen in the player, or they can subscribe. I give them a reason to subscribe: "to get new episodes automatically downloaded."

When a visitor clicks the *subscribe* link, it brings up instructions showing them exactly how to subscribe. At the very least, you should show them how to subscribe in iTunes, since it is the most popular aggregator and iPods are the most commonly used mp3 player. The handwritten font catches the visitor's attention. Another thing I suggest, if possible, is to include an audio or video explanation of your podcast and how to subscribe.

You might be wondering why I offer a streaming media player if I want visitors to subscribe. My philosophy is to allow them to get my content as easily as possible. That is what will ultimately draw them in and make them a fan. I can invite them to subscribe as time goes on.

The player in the figure above is called FeedPlayer (`feedplayer.com`). Podcast Pickle has a free player for you to use on your site at `www.podcastpickle.com/app/player/free.php`. Another popular, and inexpensive, player is the PupuPlayer, which can be purchased at `www.pupuplatters.com/pupuplayer`.

Clearly post your feed address on your site. Some visitors will know what a podcast is, know they want to subscribe and just need your address to plug into a podcatcher. If they have to search for it, they'll give up and leave.

Another great way to facilitate conversion is to post auto subscription links for some of the most popular aggregators, such as iTunes and Yahoo. However, I'm not a big fan of displaying a link for every aggregator under the sun. It gets cluttered and confuses your site visitor. I suggest posting badges for 2-4 aggregators that you think are appropriate for your audience.

To create a link that automatically subscribes someone to your podcast in iTunes, precede your feed address with `itpc://`. The link address to automatically open iTunes and subscribe to The Podcasting Underground is `itpc://www.podcastingunderground.com/feed`. Of course, the person clicking the link has to have iTunes installed for it to work. You can also create a badge for auto subscription in the Yahoo podcast directory at `podcasts.yahoo.com/publish/3#badges`.

TWO MINUTES TO MAKE YOUR MARK

Let's jump into your potential listeners' shoes again. They find your site, it piques their curiosity and they want to give your show a listen. They find the conveniently placed media player and press play. What will they hear first? What kind of first impression will you make? How long will it take for them to get to the "meaty" content?

Pay particular attention to the first two minutes of each of your episodes. Two minutes is the length of preview that iTunes gives someone when they click to sample your show. In actuality you may have as little as 30-60 seconds to give a new listener a reason not to hit the stop button. If all they hear is a lengthy intro song, over-the-top sound effects or poor sound quality, they won't be sticking around.

I always start my podcasts with a "bullet point" rundown of what I'll be talking about in the show. Carefully prepare a set of mini-headlines that outline the content for that episode. Include these points at the beginning of the episode to stimulate listeners' curiosity and compel them to keep listening. Listen to the beginning of your show from the perspective of a new listener, and ask yourself if you would keep listening based on the first 30-60 seconds.

I used to listen to a podcast, which will remain anonymous, that I finally removed from my subscription list because it wasted my time. The first minute of every show was a drawn out intro song and series of sound effects that did nothing to entertain or inform. Then it chattered on for several more minutes before getting to the real content. I even knew it would eventually talk about stuff that interested me, but I didn't have the patience to wait for it. Don't waste your listener's time. Make it clear from the start that you will give them what they're looking for.

There's nothing wrong with having an intro song. There's nothing wrong with a few well-placed sound effects. But don't be self-indulgent. Think about what your audience wants, and make it apparent in the first 30-60 seconds that you're going to give it to them.

SUMMARY

To continually grow your audience, keep an eye on the results from your marketing. Figure out what's working for your show and do more of it. This requires tracking some key web statistics, such as the number of downloads each episode gets through your feed and site.

As you track the growth of your audience, keep in mind that podcasting is still in its infancy and few shows can claim to have tens of thousands of listeners. At present, even a targeted audience of a few hundred loyal listeners can be considered a strong representation for an independent podcast.

Make it easy for your site visitors to listen and subscribe to your show. Include clear instructions about how and why to listen and subscribe. Provide links to automatically subscribe them in the popular aggregators. Also, pay particular attention to the first 30-60 seconds of your show. Do they entice a new listener to keep listening?

 Multimedia Tutorials at PodcastingUniversity.org

For more help with the topics covered in this chapter, please visit: www.PodcastingUniversity.org/pyp/chapter9

You'll find multimedia tutorials on:

- Reading your web site statistics
- Tracking the number of your listeners and subscribers
- Adding a streaming audio player to your site
- Making it easy for your site visitors to subscribe to your podcast

...and more!

Promoting Your Podcast with Information Stored in Your MP3 File

THE IMPORTANCE OF ID3 TAGS (STOP THE INSANITY!)

An mp3 file contains data that specify the artist, title, track number and other similar information about the content. This information is kept in what are called ID3 tags. These tags are displayed by media players when the file is played. Commonly used ID3 tags include the following:

- Name/Title
- Artist
- Album
- Track Number
- Genre
- Composer
- Comments
- Year

If you neglect the ID3 tags, you risk losing current and potential listeners.

These tags were originally created for music files, but they can easily be adapted for use with podcast files. You should always use ID3 tags to clearly identify each podcast file. This is important for three reasons:

1. It makes it easier for your listeners to organize, find and listen to your show. Media players use the information in the tags so they can be sorted and browsed easily. If you use consistent and convenient information in your ID3 tags, your podcasts will be easier for your listeners to sort and find. It ensures that all your episodes are grouped together in their player. Not only does this increase goodwill with your audience, it makes it more likely that they'll listen regularly. Remember, it's easier to keep a current listener then to convert a new one.

    If you neglect the ID3 tags, you risk losing current and potential listeners. Your podcast will get lost in a long list of other audio files on their media players and may never be heard because it shows up with a title of "unknown" or some other "less-than-exciting" moniker. They'll forget what it is. It will likely hit their recycle bin without a listen.

    Even if they do listen, they might not know where to find more content if they don't remember where they got it. By filling out your ID3 tags using widely accepted conventions, your file will avoid getting lost in podcast limbo.

2. Your podcast is nothing more than a digital audio file floating around in cyberspace. Someone could find it in a number of places. If you don't carefully label the file with the ID3 tags, the listener might not know how to find your web site or where to get more episodes.

3. In addition, they provide another opportunity to get your podcast's name and web address in front of listeners to ensure that you stay on the forefront of their mind and that they keep coming back for more.

As you can see, ID3 tags play a role in attracting and keeping listeners. In light of this, it seems appropriate to include a discussion in this book on how to use ID3 tags properly.

Perhaps my motivations are self-serving as well. I hate it when I download a podcast that is improperly tagged, or worse, not tagged at all. I implore you to use your ID3 tags. Don't skip this step. Create a checklist so that you remember. Tear this chapter out and use it until it becomes second nature. Whatever it takes, do use the ID3 tags and be consistent with how you use them. Spare me (and your listeners) further insanity.

The problem is that podcasters can put whatever data they want in the ID3 tags, leading to as many variations in tagging as there are podcasters—even more, since some podcasters exhibit wanton carelessness and change the format of their tags with every episode. This is the bane of podcast listeners. Inconsistent tagging makes it difficult to organize, find and listen to your podcast. Your podcast files end up in different folders and listed out of order. If it's not easy for a listener to find the latest episode of your podcast in their media player, it may never be heard.

If you're not sure what I'm ranting about, download several different podcasts and load them into your MP3 player. Try browsing for each podcast file. Play the files and take note of what information, or lack of information, is displayed. Once you're ready to pull out your hair, come back and we'll finish our discussion on tags.

You need to use your ID3 tags and be consistent. Fortunately, most podcasters have adopted a set of conventions to simplify things for listeners. Let's take a look at how to edit your tags using common conventions.

An easy way to fill out ID3 tags is with iTunes, which can be downloaded for free from www.apple.com/itunes. To edit the ID3 tags in an MP3 file, open iTunes and click on *Library* in the left sidebar. If the MP3 file you want to edit does not appear in your library, select the File menu, then *Add File to Library* to add the file.

Then right-click on the podcast file you want to edit and select *Get Info*. Click on the *Info* tab. You'll see a window that contains several fields for filling in the ID3 tags. The figure below gives an example of how I fill out the ID3 tags for an episode of *Podcasting Underground*.

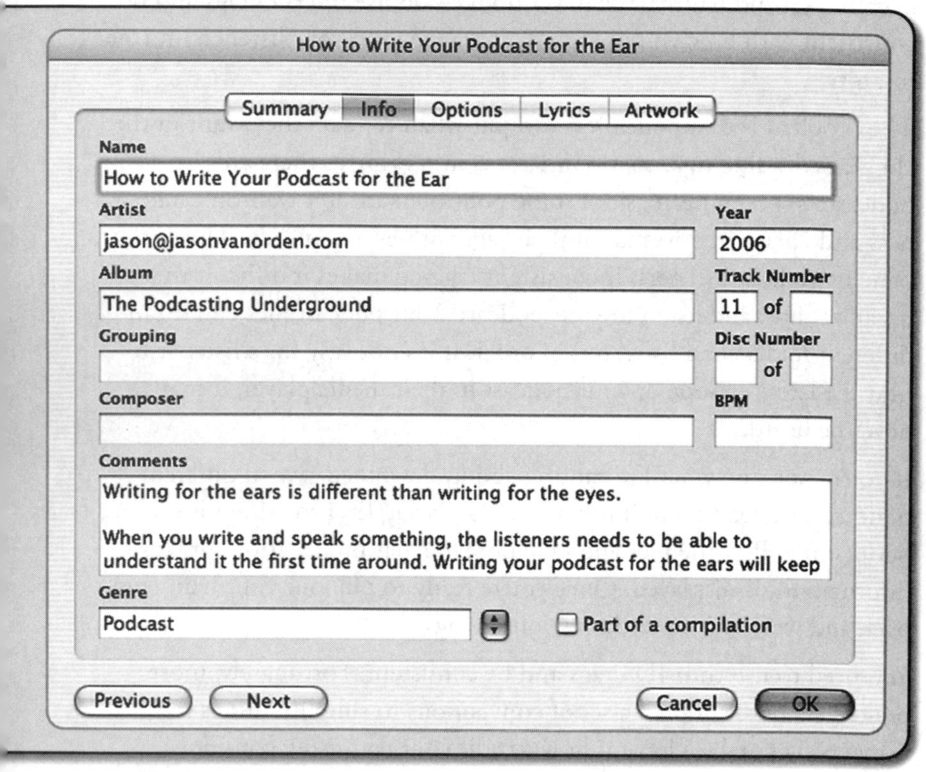

TAGGING CONVENTION

Let's take a look at what each tag means and the best convention for completing them:

Name/Title

The *Name* tag is also called *Title* in some media players. Enter the name of the episode in this tag. I also like to include the name of the podcast (or a shortened version of it such as an acronym) and the episode number or date to help identify it and list it in order with other episodes of my podcast.

The title should make it easy to determine three qualities at a glance:

> 1. What the episode is called or about
> 2. Where the episode falls in order relative to your other podcasts, making it easy for listeners to choose which episode they want to listen to next
> 3. A reminder of what podcast the episode is from

Here are examples of how I use the title tag for each of my podcasts:

- IBM#2—The Magic of Controlling Time
- GothamCast#8—Jewish Deli Smackdown
- TPU#7—Feedburner: How and Why to Use It

Artist
Usually this is the name of the host or creator of the podcast. You can also use your email here. It identifies you and reminds your listeners of how to contact you. Again, be consistent. Choose something and stick with it. Otherwise, your podcasts could end up in several different folders (annoying your listeners), because some media payers and aggregators organize files in folders by artist name.

Album
Most podcasters put the name of their podcast for the album (e.g., Podcasting Underground). I use my web address, because it contains the name of my podcast. I want to be sure the listener sees where they can go to get more episodes or show notes.

Track Number
This is where you put the episode number. When your listeners sort your podcasts by track number, the episodes will be listed in chronological order.

Composer

More than likely you'll fill this out cimilarly to the artist tag. It may seem redundant, but occasionally a media player uses this info. It's a good idea to fill it in. You can also use it to list co-creators or co-authors of your content, even if they're not hosting or speaking in the episode.

Comments

In the comments field I enter a summary of what's in the episode. This is usually a reduced version of my show notes. The comments are visible in some media players on computers and may be used more often on portable MP3 players in the near future.

Genre

There is a list of common genres available, but these are all geared for music. Some tag editors, such as iTunes, let you enter your own genre. Most podcasters enter podcast for the genre. This one is especially important. Having all the podcast files identified with this genre helps separate them from music or other types of content. Again, this is a matter of convenience for your listener.

Year

This should be self-explanatory. Some podcasters leave it blank. It's not as critical. If your content is not time sensitive and you don't want to "date" it, I can understand leaving it blank.

SUMMARY

MP3 files contain data in them that specify the artist, album, track number and other similar information that is displayed by media players. These tags were created for music files, but can easily be adapted for use with your podcast. The tags play an important part in making the listening experience a good one for your audience.

By using the ID3 tags, your listeners will be able to more easily organize, browse, find and listen to your episodes. This helps keep your audience coming back for more. It's important to be consistent and use established formats when completing ID3 tags. These tags also provide another way to get your name and web address in front of people. Repeat after me: Don't skip the tags!

Multimedia Tutorials at PodcastingUniversity.org

For more help with the topics covered in this chapter, please visit: www.PodcastingUniversity.org/pyp/chapter10

You'll find multimedia tutorials on:

- How to edit the ID3 tags in your mp3 files
- How to properly tag your files
- How to add your logo to mp3 files

...and more!

Make Some Noise

This book should have provided you with enough ideas to keep you busy for a while. The key is to set aside some time on a regular basis to plan and execute your marketing goals for your podcast. I know how it is: it may be the last thing you want to do. You're a podcaster, dangit, not a marketer! You just want to create your show. But I don't think you would have made it this far in the book if you didn't really want to see your audience grow.

My hope is that the task of promoting your podcast will seem a lot less daunting (and maybe even a little exciting) now that you are armed with an arsenal of promotional techniques that work. It will take some time and effort, but if you are patient and persevere, it will pay off in spades.

There's nothing better as a podcaster than to see your numbers go up and up and up. You'll get more feedback from your fans telling you how much they love your show. They'll eat up every word you say. They'll look to you as an expert. You'll enjoy your own little slice of celebrity.

Be creative with what you have learned in this book. Take these concepts and put your own spin on them. Let me know how it goes. You can contact me through my site at www.jasonvanorden.com. I'd love to hear your success story and even post it on my site.

I have a blog there where I offer tips and commentary on podcasting. You can also get more podcasting tips from my show, Podcasting Underground (www.podcastingunderground.com). Finally, if you want more no-holds-barred podcasting information and tutorials, be sure to check out the special offer located immediately after this chapter to get 60 days of free access to Podcasting University.

Your audience is waiting. Get out there and make some noise, because they will listen!

From: Jason Van Orden
Re: Special Reader Bonus...

Get 60 Days of FREE Access to PodcastingUniversity.org
A Bonus Worth Many Times The Cost of This Book

Now that you've read my podcast promotion tips, you can look over my shoulder and SEE how it's done.

As a purchaser of this book you are eligible for a very special offer—60 days of free access to the Podcasting University website. **Two months of access to these tutorials is worth many times the cost of this book!** It's like getting your money back, plus more.

You can get access right now by visiting this special web address:

`http://www.PodcastingUniversity.org/pypbonus`

After reading *Promoting Your Podcast*, you're armed with more promotional strategies than you'll need to make your show successful, but I know it's still easier to master something new if you see it done first. That's why I wanted to offer you this special bonus. And the resources aren't limited to podcast promotion.

Podcasting University features video and audio tutorials on all facets of podcasting... from production to making money.

These are hands-on multimedia tutorials and resources that walk you through the whole podcasting process, step by step. If you don't have a podcast yet, this will help you get one launched fast. If you already have your own show, Podcasting U will help you take things to the next level.

From XML feeds to audio compression, podcasting is full of tech jargon and pitfalls that get in the way of your creative genius. The easily accessible information in Podcasting University will help you avoid frustration and allow you to spend your time doing what you enjoy most—creating content and connecting with your audience.

PODCASTING UNIVERSITY

http://www.PodcastingUniversity.org

You'll get access to tutorials covering how to:

- Choose and set up your podcasting gear
- Record and edit your podcast to get the best audio and production quality
- Find and plan new content for your site
- Make money with your podcast
- Use podcasting to promote your business, find new customer leads
  ...and much more.

It's like having me there to show you how I do it myself.

If you hired me for a one-on-one consultation, it would cost hundreds of dollars. But now you get the next best thing for free... for two whole months!

Podcasting is a lot of fun, but the technical aspects result in a steep learning curve. If you're not an experienced audio engineer or software programmer, it will be frustrating and take a lot longer than you think. I created Podcasting University as a central place for beginning as well as advanced podcasters to get the latest podcasting information and techniques.

I'm constantly updating the university with exclusive tips and resources. Claim your free 60 days of access to Podcasting University now by visiting the following web address:

http://www.PodcastingUniversity.org/pypbonus

I look forward to seeing you at Podcasting U.

Make some noise!

Jason Van Orden

Jason Van Orden
Founder of Podcasting University & Podcasting Consultant

P.S. Just think. You're not left alone now to sort through all this info on your own. If you run into a snag, you can just hop on to the Podcasting U website for detailed help. Enroll now. What have you got to lose?

GLOSSARY

AGGREGATOR

A program or online service that checks a set of feeds (e.g., news, podcasts, blogs, etc.) and collects new items as they are posted. This makes it easy for the user to subscribe to, and gather content from, a variety of different sources. Some aggregators are programs installed on a desktop computer, and others are web-based services. Aggregators are also called feed readers, newsreaders or—in the case of podcast feed aggregation—podcatchers.

AUDIOBLOG

A weblog (see below) that consists primarily of audio content made available for streaming or download. Audioblogs are considered predecessors to podcasts. The difference with podcasting is that the audio is made available in the feed. On an audioblog it is only available on the web site.

BANDWIDTH

The measurement of how much data is uploaded to, or downloaded from, a web site. Most web hosts place a daily or monthly limit on a web site's bandwidth. This is an important issue for podcasters who offer large files for download on their sites, requiring large amounts of bandwidth.

BIT RATE

The rate at which digital data is transmitted. In reference to an mp3 file, this is measured in kilobits per second (kbps) and is an indication of how much the audio has been compressed. Higher mp3 compression yields a lower bit rate, lesser sound quality and a smaller file.

BLOG

(see weblog)

FEED

A file that summarizes web content (often for weblogs or news websites), allowing it to be syndicated on another site or aggregated by a feed reader. The feed file usually is written using a prescribed format, such as RSS or Atom.

FEEDBURNER

A service that provides a number of valuable features—such as statistics and format conversion—for blog or podcast feed publishers. Their web address is www.feedburner.com.

FORUM

An online service or community for open discussion of a given topic or theme. It is also often referred to as a discussion forum or message board.

FTP (FILE TRANSFER PROTOCOL)

A method of transferring files across the Internet, usually used to post new pages or files to a web site.

HTML (HYPERTEXT MARKUP LANGUAGE)

A markup language—consisting of a fixed set of markup tags—used to define the layout (e.g., fonts, images, links, etc.) of a web page.

ID3 TAG

Data in an mp3 file that describe the audio content, including title, artist, genre, album, year, comment and track number. The data are usually read and displayed by media players. These tags can be used by podcasters to include information about their podcast in the audio file for each episode.

MP3

A digital audio file format that has become popular on the Internet for offering music and other audio content. The format compresses the audio content and reduces the size of the audio file, by as much as ten times or more. It is the most common file format used by podcasters.

PING

A means of notification between two web sites on the Internet. When a new post is made to a weblog, the blog program can ping (notify) blog directories to let them know new content is available for listing.

PODCAST

Audio or video content made available for syndication and download through an RSS feed, making it convenient for consumers to receive the content and to listen or watch when, and how, they choose.

PODCATCHER

A type of aggregator used to subscribe to, receive and organize podcasts.

RSS (REALLY SIMPLE SYNDICATION)

A format used on the Internet to create content feeds that can be syndicated on other sites or collected by an aggregator.

URL (UNIFORM RESOURCE LOCATOR)

A web address for a web page or other file on the Internet.

WEBLOG

A type of web site that usually consist of chronological posts made by the author. The subject matter is usually some kind of news or commentary. It is also a popular way to publish a podcast.

INDEX

APPENDIX

17 MORE IDEAS FOR PROMOTING YOUR PODCAST

1. Include a tagline and link for your podcast in the signature of all of your emails.

2. Create business cards and pass them out at trade shows related to your niche (and everywhere else, for that matter).

3. Include an "email this episode" feature on your site.

4. Add your podcast and mp3s to Google Base (base.google.com).

5. Join or create a podcasters association in your area.

6. Offer free seminars or presentation on your niche topic.

7. Join an online network or community of podcasts that relate to your topic.

8. Run a Google Adwords or Overture campaign.

9. Create postcards and place them around businesses that your potential listeners are likely to frequent.

10. Burn CDs of your show and hand them out to people that are likely to enjoy your show. Remember to label the CD with all the info pertinent to your podcast.

11. Submit your web site to web directories.

12. Interview someone who has a large list of clients/customers/fans that they are likely to tell about the show.

13. Attend a local club/association related to your topic; network with people and pass out business cards or flyers.

14. Start a MySpace page for your podcast. Network with friends who have similar interests.

15. Buy a text ad in an email newsletter that goes out to your target audience.

16. Collect testimonials from your listeners and use them on your site and with your marketing.

17. Regularly create fantastic content that people will want to listen to, talk about and share with their friends.

Not For Dummies

When You Need The Advanced Level Information

AT A BOOKSTORE NEAR YOU

![Don't Miss the Podcasting Boat!](crowded boat scene)

///Don't Miss the Podcasting Boat!

Podcasting is today's hottest marketing tool. If you're not Podcasting, you're missing out on a huge opportunity to connect with more prospects and customers at a more intimate level. But as you've discovered by reading this book—production work on a Podcast takes time, effort and expertise. That's why Larstan has developed a complete Podcasting production service.

Larstan Podcast Production Service Includes:
» State-of-the-art production/recording studio with digital editing
» Complete program planning and production, including "show clock"
» Special effects library
» Custom music for intros, outros and bridges
» Call-in/phone interview capability
» Syndication to leading Podcast directories including Yahoo and iTunes
» Development of a unique website to accompany your show
» Subscriber tracking reports

Special Offer—For Readers Only!
Mention that you read Promoting Your Podcast book and receive 50% off your first podcast.

For more information contact:
Larstan Podcasting Production Department
240-396-0007 x905
jremondini@larstan.net
www.larstan.com

LARSTAN Podcasting